T0329436

VIDOKONI :
Folktales from Mzimba, Malawi

Harvey C. Chidoba Banda

Langaa Research & Publishing CIG
Mankon, Bamenda

Publisher:

Langaa RPCIG
Langaa Research & Publishing Common Initiative Group
P.O. Box 902 Mankon
Bamenda
North West Region
Cameroon
Langaagrp@gmail.com
www.langaa-rpcig.net

Distributed in and outside N. America by African Books Collective
orders@africanbookscollective.com
www.africanbookscollective.com

ISBN: 9956-763-84-5

DISCLAIMER
All views expressed in this publication are those of the author and do
not necessarily reflect the views of Langaa RPCIG.

Dedication

For

Owen:

Banyinu bakulemba mabuku: imwe mungalemba?

(Your colleagues are able to write books: can you?)

About the Book

This book makes a rare contribution towards the preservation and promotion of *ukhaliro wa bene Malawi* (Malawian culture) that is fast waning. This dilution of culture was put in motion by the British colonial masters and got exacerbated with the inception of democratic governance in 1994. There is need for concerted efforts amongst various practitioners and stakeholders, led by the government itself, if the situation is to be put under control. Otherwise, sooner or later, it will simply be remote history that 'long time ago, there was a unique culture in Malawi'. The book is a collection of twenty short stories that generally promote such themes as *nkharo yiwemi* (good behaviour); *uheni wa chigolo na sanje* (the bad side of selfishness and jealousy); *kulimbikira pa vinthu* (hard working spirit); and *uheni wa mitala* (the folly of polygamy), among others. The strength of the book lies in the fact that there is room for the reader to draw their own lessons based on their understanding of a particular story, in addition to the lesson already highlighted there-in. The book is a must read for all, young and old, especially those interested in understanding the societal values, not only about Malawi, but of Africa as a whole.

About the Author

Harvey C. Chidoba Banda was born on 10th August 1975 in Mzimba district in northern Malawi. He attended primary schools in Mzimba, Nkhata-Bay and Rumphi districts before being selected to Livingstonia Secondary School in 1991. Between 1996 and 2000 he obtained a Bachelor of Education (Humanities) from Chancellor College, a constituent college of the University of Malawi. In 2008 he obtained a Master of Arts (African Social History) from the same institution. After working briefly at Kasungu Secondary School and Domasi College of Education, he joined Mzuzu University in 2006 as a Lecturer in African History in the Department of History, where he served as Head of Department between 2009 and 2013. Harvey is married to Jennifer Luhanga and they have one child, Owen.

About the Composer

Harry Chidoba Banda, the author's father, was born in 1944 in Mzimba district. He is married to Edith Njikho also from the same district and they have seven children: three boys and four girls. Harry worked as a Civil Servant in several Departments mainly in northern Malawi and retired in 1995. It was only during his retirement that he began to nurture his natural and in-born talent that had been dormant for a long time: acting! He started composing songs and short drama pieces and used to be engaged by Non-Governmental Organisations in Mzimba district. It is his wish to have some of his works documented for posterity that culminated into this book.

Table of Contents

xi

Acknowledgements

Joey Power rightly argues in her book *Political Culture and Nationalism in Malawi: Building Kwacha* that writing a book is a solitary and selfish pursuit. Consequently, it naturally incurs huge debts. I am greatly indebted to Mzuzu University Management for granting me study leave for PhD studies at the University of the Witwatersrand. It was only during this time that I was able to squeeze into my busy academic schedules to complete the 'unfinished business.' More importantly, I would like to express my heart-felt gratitude to my father, Harry Chidoba Banda, for composing these *vidokoni* from scratch. Despite his rare talent, this might have been a daunting task, considering his age! To be quite candid, without his part there could have been no such book as this one. If I were to liken this symbiotic relationship to gardening, *iwo bakapanga mizere apo ine nkhalimirira waka!* (he made the ridges while I merely did the weeding!)

In addition, I would like to thank the Secretary in the Department of History at Mzuzu University, Mrs Ireen Kondowe, for typing the entire manuscript, quite a distraction from her personal and daily schedules. Credit also goes to the reviewers and publishers for their immense contribution towards the process of refining unclear and, in some cases, utterly vague 'formulations.' However, all errors in this book, be they of commission or omission, remain my sole responsibility.

Above all, I am singularly grateful to my wife, Jennifer, for her encouragement and unwavering support throughout this book project, and to my son, Owen, for his incessant curiosity: when is the book coming out? Such questions like this one were the engine that propelled the entire project. It is, therefore, in order that I dedicate this book to him!

Preface

This book, a short 'memoir,' is a collection of folktales (short stories) smartly coined and vividly narrated by my father, Harry Chidoba Banda. I have translated them almost exclusively in literal form. It is worth noting that I have had the onerous task of intelligibly and, I hope, convincingly presenting these stories (in two separate books though) in both English and *Chitumbuka* (vernacular), the language of the populace in northern Malawi. The idea behind is to broaden readership, that is, to enable people of all ages (young and old) and of all categories (literate and otherwise) read them with understanding. It is important again to emphasize the fact that the value of these stories is to be found in the meaning and lessons that each of them carries. In short, the stories should not be read as mere 'newspaper stories.' Instead, while reading them the readers should endeavour to probe their deeper meaning and lessons to be drawn in each case. The ultimate aim behind these stories is to help in moulding good citizenry with upright character befitting the societal and cultural expectations of not only democratic Malawi, but, indeed, of other societies far and wide!

Malawi is a small, agricultural and land-locked country in south-central Africa bordering Tanzania to the north; Mozambique to the south and east; and Zambia to the west. It was under the British colonial (mal) administration up to 1964 when it attained independence. Like in most parts of Africa, the British tended to impose their way of life on the people they governed. As a result and with the passage of time, local people tended to think, wrongly though, that 'everything white was good while everything black or African was bad.' This consequently led to the dilution and, in some cases, utter abandonment, as it were, of the traditional customs, values and cultures. The latter here simply means the African way of life. In the Malawian context, this would locally be described as *ukhaliro wa bene Malawi* (in *Chitumbuka* the dominant language of northern Malawi) and *chikhalidwe cha a Malawi* (in *Chichewa* dominant in central and southern Malawi). It is this that was at stake!

In the case of Malawi, the one-party regime under the tutelage of Dr. Hastings Kamuzu Banda should be commended for the unique role it played in trying to preserve these traditional and cultural values. However, this does not imply that Dr. Banda's regime was without blemish. In fact, it scored fearfully low on the natural freedoms and the human rights front. No wonder it came under heavy fire and was forced to pave way for the multi-party and democratic politics in 1994. This was following the wind of change that blew across most African countries in the early 1990s.

The inception of democracy in Malawi, though in itself a good thing, was associated with a host of ills in society. People exercised the all-along scarce freedoms and human rights to the full. However, sooner or later, there was moral degeneration and decay in society. The Malawian values were, once again, thrown to the dogs! People generally misinterpreted these freedoms and human rights. People defended whatever they were doing even if it was wrong, arguing 'it is my right and I am free to do what I please!'

It is at this juncture that concern at the societal level crept in, particularly with the erosion of the once-precious Malawian cultural values. It is against this background that books that border on culture like *Vidokoni: Folktales from Mzimba, Malawi* are most valuable. Their significance in this respect cannot be overemphasised: they are there to assist in the preservation and promotion of the traditional customs, values and norms unashamedly being swamped aside! This book (English version) is accompanied by another version in *Chitumbuka* in order to broaden readership among the Malawian populace.

Harvey C. Chidoba Banda
Witwatersrand University, 2015

Chapter 1
Mungaja

Long time ago, there lived two people, a husband and his wife. This couple had a daughter named Mungaja. This daughter had a habit of stealing items from her parents' house. Whenever the mother interrogated her "Are you the one who has eaten part of the relish?," for instance, she used to say 'no'. This kept on happening and continued as the order of the day and her parents used to complain bitterly about the loss of numerous items from the household.

At one time her mother kept some groundnuts in a sealed clay pot as seed for the next growing season. Day by day the parents used to check the pot to see to it that it had not been tampered with. This used to happen until the planting season came.

One day Mungaja's parents went to the garden to prepare ridges with the hope that, once enough, they should use the stored groundnuts to plant in these ridges. But alas! When the mother returned from the field, she found that her daughter had actually invited her friends over, broken the pot open, and had eaten almost all the groundnuts contained therein, with left-overs scattered all-over. In fact, it had been more or less like a feast!

Her mother literally cried out loud, bereaving that all the seed they had collected for a long time (months on end) and hoped to plant was gone in a flash. Her mother asked her, "Are you again going to refute that you are not the one who has eaten the stored groundnuts?" To be quite candid, Mungaja had no befitting answer. The mother later reported the matter to her husband (Mungaja's father) and told him how Mungaja, in the company of her equally-mischievous friends, had eaten all the groundnut seed. Upon hearing the news and, at the same time, realizing that they had laboured in vain, that is, they prepared ridges only to realize there was no seed to plant, her father became so furious that he declared that she was no longer allowed to stay in their household. Instead, the father instructed her mother to dump Mungaja in an old, dilapidated and collapsing house in their earlier settlement place, locally termed *manquba*. Mungaja was to stay and remain there for the rest of her life.

So it happened. Mungaja was abandoned in a deserted 'forest'. Mungaja's mother and her aunt were filled with sorrow and heart-felt sadness because of this development. However, there was nothing they could have done realizing that this was a culmination of a series of little thefts committed by Mungaja. The one painful thing in all this was the continued refutation by Mungaja, maintaining she had not committed the offence (theft at hand).

In a dramatic move to show motherly love and without the knowledge of Mungaja's father, her mother and aunt solemnly agreed to provide Mungaja with part of the food they were preparing in their respective households, as part of her upkeep. But the two knew pretty well that her father would not take kindly to such an agreement, hence their determination to keep this a secret. The two 'mothers' were above all concerned about Mungaja's health, knowing pretty well too that without food Mungaja would surely die. They were determined to keep her alive, at least.

The first time the two visited Mungaja, they knocked at her door and sang in unison: "Mungaja open the door, you have been locked out because of groundnut seed!" Upon recognizing their voices, she opened the door for them. Thereafter, they could give her the food, chat with her for some time and later bid farewell. After they left, she could lock herself inside. It is worth noting that the locks were so strong that even the hyena could not open to devour Mungaja.

They instructed her to master the voice of her mother and aunt, independently, because the two, thereafter, would be visiting her separately. It was only these who were to visit her as the father had no concern whatsoever about Mungaja's predicament. They further instructed her not to open the door once she heard a male voice because, for sure, her father was not going to visit her anyway.

At this juncture, it is worth noting that Mungaja personally knew she was in the wrong depicted in her response to her mother's and aunt's knocking at her door and her saying: "Indeed, mother, indeed aunt, you have locked me out because of groundnut seed!"

One day a hyena came to know that in this dilapidated house lived a young girl named Mungaja. Hence the hyena wanted to go one day and try to knock with the hope that once Mungaja opened for him (hyena), then he could devour her. Despite knocking, Mungaja never opened the door for hyena because his voice was conspicuously different from her mother's and aunt's voices. Having failed, hyena decided to visit a *sing'anga* (herbalist) to look for a way to follow in order to get after Mungaja. Hyena explained to *sing'anga* that he sings just like the mother and aunt at Mungaja's door, but to no avail. The *sing'anga* asked hyena "what kind of voice do you use when singing?" Hyena answered "I sing using my hyena voice." The *sing'anga* requested hyena to rehearse the song. Hyena retorted: "Mungaja, open the door, you have

3

been locked outside because of groundnuts." (He sang using a very deep, audible voice). The *sing'anga* told hyena that with such a deep, male voice there was no way Mungaja would open the door for him. He, therefore, advised hyena to imitate the voices of Mungaja's mother and aunt. This is exactly what hyena did.

Eventually, after mastering the voices, hyena went alone and knocked at Mungaja's door while singing: "Mungaja open the door, you have locked me outside because of groundnuts." At first Mungaja hesitated: "Is this my mother's voice?" "It must definitely be aunt's voice," she concluded. She, therefore, responded accordingly: "Indeed, aunt, you have locked me outside because of groundnuts." The moment she opened the door, hyena grabbed her, and immediately started eating her body, killing Mungaja in the process. By the time Mungaja's mother arrived to give her food, the door was wide open and there was blood all over the place. When she came closer, she discovered her daughter's head lying on the ground. The rest of the body was missing.

The people in the village were surprised to see Mungaja's mother coming from the bush and, simultaneously, crying uncontrollably, saying: "Oh, my daughter what a way to die – being devoured by a beast (hyena)!" As a result of this, everyone in the village, including people from the adjacent villages, came to learn about Mungaja's painful death. In the end, her family members, in the company of other villagers, collected Mungaja's head and buried it in the family's graveyard, as is the norm. It was a painful and saddening death, indeed.

The lesson to be drawn from this short story, especially for the young and the youth, is that when you are staying with your parents refrain from stealing items, however small they may be. If you resort to stealing, you will do exactly like what Mungaja used to do: refuting that she had not stolen any item from the household, when, in fact, the opposite was true. If this habit continues, you may even start stealing from other people's households, becoming a full-fledged thief in the process.

You may wish to know that this may have dire consequences. For instance, once you are caught stealing, you may be killed in the process or you may be handed over to the police, who may, in turn, hand you over to the court authorities. Once you are found guilty, you may be given a tough jail sentence – serving in prison for a specified period. What is worse is that even after release from prison, you tend to lose respect which the society normally accords a person. Whenever you do something wrong, even if it is by mistake, this is the kind of societal response that you get: "What else do you expect from an ex-convict?" In most cases, the people's perception is that prison is a place where one 'loses his or her head'.

You have learnt from the story that Mungaja was actually abandoned and locked out in the bush as a result of her stealing habits. Following this she ended up being killed by a hyena. Whenever you want anything from your parent's households, be it groundnuts, maize, cassava, you name it, make sure you ask your parents and avoid stealing under any circumstance.

There is an old adage which says *unkhungu ukukomeska* ("stealing leads one to death"). This is really true. From this story alone we have seen how incessant stealing can lead to a very demeaning and painful death – being eaten by a hyena!

An elderly woman at her home preparing meat for relish as her granddaughter looks on. (photo by author)

Chapter 2
Njala Nkhakoko

L ong time ago, there were three people: a man (*dada*), his wife (*muboli wake*) and their daughter-in-law (*mkamwana*), that is, the wife to their son. In this story the man is called Kawenjelele, the wife nyaNdhlovu (nee Ndhlovu) and *mkamwana* nyaMtonga (nee Mtonga). This family had two gardens, one for the couple and the second one for *mkamwana*. They grew millet in both gardens.

In the couple's millet garden, they had a good, healthy crop - the millet grew so tall that someone could even harvest while standing. Contrariwise, in nyaMtonga's garden the millet was stunted. This was partly as a result of 'overcrowding' of the seed during sowing. As a result of this, nyaMtonga was worried in her heart, realizing the tough job ahead of her when harvesting such stunted millet. She therefore started looking for a mechanism of how to exchange their millet gardens. However, she could not air out her thoughts to the couple. This was aggravated by the fact that, traditionally, nyaMtonga was supposed to observe distance from her *tatavyala* (father-in-law). In fact, she was not even supposed to talk to him directly.

As a solution to the problem, nyaMtonga composed a song which goes:

"Kambombo wali kumunda wane,
vimakoyobola vili kwa amama.
Nadandaula ine amama,
Kambombo wali kumunda wane,

7

vimakoyobola vili kwa amama.
Nalila ine amama."

("There is *kambombo* (stunted millet) in my garden,
makoyobola (healthy millet) in my mother's garden.
Mother, I am grieving.
There is *kambombo* in my garden,
makoyobola in my mother's garden.
Mother, I am crying.")

NyaMtonga used to sing this song whenever she was
pounding in order to draw the attention of her *tatavyala*
(father-in-law) and *mamavyala* (mother-in-law). She wanted
them to know that the stunted millet in her garden, which she
referred to as *kambombo*, was a concern to her, particularly
that she could not manage to harvest all the millet in her
garden since it is generally rigorous and tiresome to harvest
kambombo. At the same time, she wanted the two to know that
she preferred harvesting *makoyobola* (healthy millet) in their
garden. *Makoyobola* is relatively easier to harvest since you can
harvest the millet upright (while standing), hence less tiring.
Time and again, whenever she was pounding, she used to sing
the song: "In my garden there is *kambombo*, while *makoyobola*
in *mamavyala's* garden."

One day when nyaMtonga was singing the same song
while pounding maize, Kawenjelele asked her wife: "My wife,
do you know why *mkamwana* sings this song whenever she is
pounding?" His wife responded: "No, not at all. I have always
thought it is the normal kind of singing which women do
when pounding." She continued: "In fact, I am saying this
because I have never quarrelled with *mkamwana* and even her
mlamu (sister-in-law), Njalayabo, has never quarrelled with

8

her. Had it been that we ever quarrelled, we would have thought that may be that is why she sings like that." Kawenjelele, the husband, told her that nyaMtonga's aim behind such singing was because she would like the two sides to exchange their millet fields – "nyaMtonga to get our garden with *makoyobola*, while we get hers with *kambombo*." Kawenjelele continued, emphatically: "I can assure you that once this is done nyaMtonga will be very happy and, in fact, she will stop singing this song while pounding."

Consequently, nyaNdhlovu and her husband called nyaMtonga. This is what nyaNdhlovu said: "We have called you, your father-in-law and myself, and we want to inform you that we have decided that we should exchange our garden with yours, that you take our *makoyobola* garden and we take your *kambombo* garden." She further explained that they had realized that it would, indeed, be easier for her to harvest tall millet unlike stunted millet. But that they, themselves, were prepared to harvest *kambombo*. In addition, nyaMtonga was instructed to clap her hands to show that she was in agreement with their decision since she could not verbally respond to their proposal in the presence of her *tatayvala*. "Do you agree that we should exchange our gardens?" nyaNdhlovu asked. Soon after posing the question, they heard nyaMtonga clapping her hands *"khu khu khu!"* (sound of hand clapping). She had agreed. They therefore instructed her to start harvesting from her new *makoyobola* garden the following week. They, themselves, were to switch onto her *kambombo* garden. NyaMtonga was assured that whatever she harvested was hers and she was free to keep the millet in her *nkhokwe* (granary). "As for us, we will see how far we will go harvesting *kambombo*. The little we realize, we will keep some in our *nkhokwe*," continued nyaNdhlovu. At this point, nyaMtonga was over the moon!

So it happened, as agreed: nyaMtonga started harvesting *makoyobola* and nyaNdhlovu, with her husband, *kambombo*. It is worth noting that nyaMtonga harvested a lot of millet to the point where it could not fit into a big *nkhokwe*. They actually used *musi* (a pestle) as a presser in order to fit it in. As for *kambombo*, in line with everyone's expectation, the yield was relatively less. But the good thing was that they had no grudges against each other and lived happily together.

Within a short period of time, you may wish to know, nyaMtonga befriended a lot of ladies in the village and her friends always expected her to give them a share of the huge reserve of millet. Knowing that the millet came not from her garden, but from *mamavyala's* garden, she used to share the millet in secret. She never wanted them to know. This continued as a habit, she used to distribute the millet on a regular basis.

Guess what? By December the millet stock had run out. The millet *nkhokwe* was but empty. Consequently, nyaMtonga stayed for three consecutive days without food. Even her children slept on empty stomachs. On the fourth day she became concerned about the lives of her children. She was afraid she was going to lose them because of acute hunger. However, at the same time, she had no audacity to ask for some food from her *mamavyala's* house. She was filled with shame and guilt. She knew she had had a bumper yield and, obviously, her *mamavyala* was going to ask how all the millet (*makoyobola*) was gone within a short period of time. NyaMtonga devised a trick. She decided to send one of her children to go to her *gogo's* (grandmother's) house and ask for *visinga* (fire sticks) with which she could light fire in her house. When the daughter came with *visinga*, nyaMtonga poured water over them, extinguishing the fire in the process. The intention was that the daughter should go back to her *gogo* for yet other *visinga*, after reporting that the fire had gone out along the way. This happened three times and each time nyaMtonga deliberately put out the fire. In the end, Kawenjelele asked his wife: "Do you know the real reason as to why our *mkamwana* cannot light the fire?" NyaNdhlovu was very frank: "I don't know. Honestly, I think maybe it's because of the just-ended rain which may have soaked wet the dry grass and firewood for lighting the fire!" Her husband came in: "That's not the reason at all. The actual reason is that she has no food in her house." In order to be proven right, Kawenjelele advised his wife, nyaNdhlovu, to give nyaMtonga a pail (full) of millet and that, once done, she would light the fire and prepare food for her household. This is exactly what his wife did. "Here's a pail of millet, process it and prepare millet flour with which you should prepare food for our *bazukulu* (grand children)," she told nyaMtonga.

NyaMtonga was very thankful. For the first time, she was even forced to utter words in the presence of her *tatavyala*, contrary to tradition and culture. "Thank you very much. I am really grateful," she lamented. Thereafter, in a flash she collected the millet and went back to her house, accompanied by one of her children. Within a short period of time, she lit the fire, prepared relish from vegetables (*mphangwe*) and later prepared *sima* using millet flour. All this happened within a short while. Eventually, all the members in her household ate and *bakakhuta* (were satisfied).

Kawenjelele asked her wife, nyaNdhlovu: "Have you noticed that the problem of failing to light fire is no more?" "Exactly, you were right. The problem was that she had no food in her house and she was shy to ask for some millet, realizing that she had been extravagant in using *makoyobola* she had harvested," responded his wife.

The lesson from the story is that despite the bumper harvest, we are supposed to use the farm produce cautiously, knowing pretty well that once we are careless and extravagant, we will quickly run out of stock. The result is that we will be victims of untold hunger. This is exactly what nyaMtonga experienced. However, this was a problem which she created for herself and which could, surely, have been avoided.

There is a saying that *"moto panyumba ntchakurya"* (food necessitates fire lighting). If there are no foodstuffs in the house there is virtually no need to light the fire. You actually light the fire if you have something to cook or prepare. Otherwise, it does not make sense. In the same vein, there is also another saying which goes *"njala nkhakoko"* ("hunger is more of a beast"). You have seen how, because of hunger, nyaMtonga was continually putting out the fire because there was no food to prepare for her household. By putting out the fire, nyaMtonga wanted her *mamavyala* to realize, on her own volition, the need to provide her with some foodstuffs amidst acute food shortage. However, nyaMtonga realised that she found herself trapped in this predicament because of her own carelessness.

Bana (children) having fun at home; a sign that they have eaten and all is well in the household. (photo by author)

Chapter 3
Mitala

Long time ago there was a man named Ambuyeye. He had two wives: nyaGondwe and nyaThole. Ambuyeye had a queer habit: he would spend the night at nyaGondwe's house and then early the next morning he would leave for nyaThole's house, where he would demand warm water for a bath and also porridge. NyaThole was obliged to provide these two. NyaGondwe, at the same time, would prepare warm water and porridge realizing that her husband needed these in the morning. She was often shocked, however, to hear "I have already taken a bath at nyaThole's house" from her husband. "Okay, if you have already bathed, here's porridge as your breakfast," nyaGondwe would continue. Only to be told: "I have also already taken breakfast, porridge."

This used to happen time and again. At times it could be nyaThole preparing water and breakfast and at other times it was nyaGondwe. In the process, each was being forced to throw away food because their husband could not eat, having already eaten at a different place. The two wives noticed that they were wasting a lot of foodstuffs in the process. However, neither one of them had the audacity to confront their husband for fear of being beaten, at least, and being chased away, at most. The latter option could actually mean the end of marriage. Ambuyeye's unbecoming habit continued until the two wives got really fed up.

It was quite clear Ambuyeye did not know to conduct himself *mnyumba ya mitala* (in a polygamous family). Consequently, nyaGondwe and nyaThole agreed on a deal.

They decided to engage a bird to rebuke their husband, Ambuyeye, through singing. By singing loudly day and night, the bird was to bring about tension and unrest in the village, in the process drawing the attention and wrath of the village headman. The bird used to sing this song:

> *"Ambuyeye, Ambuyeye, kugona*
> *mwagona kunyake, kugeza*
> *mwageza kunyake, kurya*
> *mwarya kunyake, mulije*
> *kuyimanya mitala, Ambuyeye*
> *mulije kuyimanya mitala, Ambuyeye."*

("Ambuyeye, Ambuyeye,
sleeping, you have slept at a different place
bathing, you have bathed at a different place
eating, you have eaten at a different place.
You don't know proper conduct in polygamy, Ambuyeye,
You don't know proper conduct in polygamy, Ambuyeye.")

The village headman got furious and instructed his people to lie in waiting (ambush) and grab and bring forward the person who was causing sleepless nights through noise. So the people did as instructed: they managed to catch the bird. Upon interrogation, the bird revealed that it was not out of its own volition; rather it was following a humble request from nyaGondwe and nyaThole, who were bent on exposing the unbecoming and discomforting behaviour of Ambuyeye, their husband. The bird explained to the captors that the two women were concerned about the food that was being wasted almost on a daily basis. Their expectation was that if their husband spent a night at nyaGondwe's house, he was supposed to do everything there, including bathing and taking breakfast the following morning before moving to nyaThole's house, if he wanted to do so.

The village headman sent his *nduna* (assistant) to summon Ambuyeye for interrogation. The chief wanted to find out whether the allegations levelled against Ambuyeye were correct or not. "Is it true that once you spend a night at nyaGondwe's house, the following morning you leave for nyaThole's place, where you take a bath and breakfast?" asked the village headman. "Indeed, that is what I always do. Similarly, when I spend a night at nyaThole's house, I go to nyaGondwe's house where I ask for warm bathing water and porridge," responded Ambuyeye, as if what he was doing was right. "In fact, I always make sure I take breakfast before I depart for beer drinking during the day," continued Ambuyeye, unashamedly. "Why do you do this, if I may ask?" interrupted the village headman. "Simple. I do that because they are both my wives. I don't see any problem with that!" responded Ambuyeye, without any remorse.

In the process, the elders of the village advised him that that was not how he was supposed to behave and conduct himself in a polygamous household. They further explained to him that, usually, where you spend a night you are supposed to bathe and take breakfast there the next morning. In fact, you are supposed to stay there for the entire week before moving to the other wife's place. It means that a whole week is one wife's turn to look after her husband, in totality. Ambuyeye was eventually rebuked for bringing about confusion and unnecessary animosity between his wives, and also wastage with regard to foodstuffs.

The lesson from this story is simple: whoever is in polygamy is supposed to make sure that he does everything at the wife's place where he has spent a night or is spending nights. This is supposed to be the case until such a time you switch onto your other wife's place. This includes all the household activities: if it is going to the garden, you will go to the garden of the wife where you are resident for that time. This is supposed to be the case, always, to prevent squabbles and bickering between wives.

Even nowadays this is how men who have polygamous families behave. Otherwise, there will be no peace in the two households. The latter will always be characterised by tension, animosity, and hatred, to mention but some.

Chapter 4
Kamuzunguzeni na Chimbwe

Long time ago, there lived a very poor woman. Her poverty was exposed all the more when she gave birth to a child named Kamuzunguzeni. The mother could not even afford a *chitenje* (wrapper) with which to wrap her child on her back, rightfully called *ngubo*. She was deeply troubled in her heart; she did not know how she was going to proceed without a *chitenje*.

She eventually decided to borrow some money with which to buy *ngubo*. However, most people she approached lamented that they, too, had financial constraints. Some were simply dismissive by saying they did not have money. Looking at the plight of Kamuzunguzeni's mother, they thought that, if they lent her money, she would not pay back.

One day, she approached hyena for the assistance in question. "Please lend me one *nyanda* (another expression for *chitenje*; specifically a piece of cloth) so that I should use it in wrapping my child at my back?" she asked. In response, hyena said: "I have lots of *nyanda* so I can easily lend you one, but my concern is simple: if I do that, how will you pay back since it is clear you are one of the very poor in this village?" Kamuzunguzeni's mother told hyena that once Kamuzunguzeni grew into adulthood (manhood) and after assisting his mother in various ways, material and otherwise, she would hand him over to hyena as "pay back" and hyena would be free to eat her child, Kamuzunguzeni.

Hyena quickly got interested and gave her the *nyanda* she asked for. Hyena did not hesitate knowing of the big repayment at hand. Mother and child lived together until

19

Kamuzunguzeni came of age. Realizing that his mother was poor, Kamuzunguzeni quickly embarked on farming. As a result, his mother's household never lacked foodstuffs (farm produce). Most people, generally, appreciated the assistance and support which he provided his mother with. The latter did not lack anything because of the support in question. In addition, he built a good house for his mother. He also used to keep all kinds of *vibeto* (livestock): *nkhuku* (chicken), *mbuzi* (goats), guinea fowl, *ng'ombe* (cattle), to name but some. These were all kept by Kamuzunguzeni.

One day, after many years, hyena approached Kamuzunguzeni's mother and enquired: "When will you pay back for the *nyanda* I lent you so many years ago?" "I am not yet ready, hyena," she replied. Hyena went back home. After staying for some time, hyena remembered that as a matter-of-fact, the mother had promised to hand over Kamuzunguzeni as pay back. Hence hyena went back for clarification. "I thought you told me that, after growing up, you would hand over to me your son, Kamuzunguzeni, as repayment for the *nyanda*?" hyena asked. "Yes, that was the agreement and I also agree now that time (in years) has passed since I got the *nyanda* in question. So, come to my house at night. I will tell Kamuzunguzeni to sleep in the living room," the mother replied. She further told hyena that she was going to impress on her son not to sleep in his usual room pretending that she was feeling unwell and would need assistance during the night – help to reach drinking water for example. "Please, make sure that you don't fail to come," she implored hyena. She further assured hyena that the door would not be locked, hence making it easy for hyena to get in. She told hyena that, once he got in, he was free to eat Kamuzunguzeni, her son, so that the long-standing debt should be settled once and for all. Little did the mother know that Kamuzunguzeni was around, on the other side of the *khonde* (veranda) during this conversation. In fact, he heard all they had agreed; how hyena was to eventually eat Kamuzunguzeni.

Hyena went back home full of happiness. In fact, for him the time was dragging, he wished for night time to come so as to fulfil the agreement. The mother told Kamuzunguzeni to sleep in the living room, not in his usual bedroom, because she was ill. Kamuzunguzeni obliged. However, he was filled with sadness, after reflecting on his mother's 'strategic plan' with the hyena. Kamuzunguzeni could hardly sleep at night, realizing that death was around the corner. Way into the night, he noticed his mother was fast asleep, he noted this from the deep, disturbing snarling coming from her bedroom. "I have done a lot for my mother since I grew up. I remember vividly my mother being very poor when I was young. After all this (all the support I have rendered to her), she goes ahead making an arrangement for my speedy death?" Kamuzunguzeni wondered. He was deeply troubled. After deep thoughts, he came to the conclusion that this was very unfair. He, therefore, devised his own counter plan (the master plan). He decided that he was going to shift his mother from the bedroom to the sitting room without her noticing. He, himself, was to take his mother's place. In fact, he never slept in his mother's bed. He did squat in the corner of the room though, awaiting the arrival of hyena in order to see his mother's fate.

When it was 10 o'clock at night hyena entered the house, salivating, full of excitement that he was going "to eat meat tonight." He jumped onto the bed and grabbed Kamuzunguzeni's mother. Before the latter could cry out "oh save me I'm dying," hyena had already dragged her out, with blood spilling all over. When hyena wanted to start eating his "catch," he realized it was a female's body. He could not understand this. He was deeply troubled: "How come this is a female's body, when I have strictly followed the instruction, that is, to catch and kill Kamuzunguzeni on the sitting room?" At the end he concluded "let me simply eat the meat since I have already killed the woman."

Early next morning people were surprised to see a stretch of blood from the house of the mother of Kamuzunguzeni all the way into the bush. They tried to call for his mother, only to see Kamuzunguzeni coming from the house. "Why are you coming from your mother's house and not your house?" "What is all this blood for?" they asked, in unison. "It is hyena which has caught and killed my mother," Kamuzunguzeni explained. And he continued "in fact, it was my mother who had a deal with hyena that he should come at night and kill me!" "What wrong have you committed?" they wondered. He explained to them how it all happened: "When I was very young, mother told me, she was very poor to buy *nyanda*, hence she secured this from hyena" on credit on the understanding that Kamuzunguzeni will later in life (adulthood) be handed over to hyena. This was to come after his mother was satisfied that Kamuzunguzeni had assisted her enough and when his mother could now stand on her own. All this was because his mother could not repay the credit. He further explained that, as he was growing up, he had realized that the only way out of poverty was hard work and that is why he worked very hard until poverty got alleviated in his and his mother's compound. For this he was very happy. However, little did he know that there was such an agreement in the background.

Kamuzunguzeni also narrated how the mother cheated on him, pretending to be sick and, therefore, being in need of assistance. This necessitated Kamuzunguzeni sleeping in the living room, close to the mother, in case she needed his assistance during the night. He told the people that his mother did not know that he was listening to every bit of their conversation. Thereafter, he clarified, he did not want to escape from the village fearing that the villagers would have thought he was the one who had instigated the whole move.

This development was later taken to *mafumu* (village headmen) for arbitration. Because of the large number of village headmen, they constituted a representative council comprising:

Inkosana Mtaja Chavula
Group Village Headman Chindiku Juma Mkandawire
Group Village Headman Chinombo Tchaya
Group Village Headman Londobala Bota
Group Village Headman Mzondi Ndhlovu
Village Headman Zoto Chavula
Village Headman Mukhosana Qumayo

The first one to speak during the deliberations was Group Village Headman Chindiku Juma Mkandawire. After going through the facts as provided by son, Kamuzunguzeni, he came to the conclusion that Kamuzunguzeni's mother "was not only hard-hearted, but also foolish," especially considering the agreement she reached with hyena as regards repayment for *nyanda*. Group Village Headman Chinombo Tchaya concurred with Group Village Headman Mkandawire on all his observations and conclusions. Tchaya continued, thus: "it would have been better if the mother mentioned, say, *ng'ombe* (cattle), *mbuzi* (goats), *mberere* (sheep), etc. as a form of repayment. She should have known better that by reaching this agreement she was bound to drift back to poverty," he continued.

Inkosana Mtaja Chavula interrupted by saying "this case does not require any of us to come in. The hard-heartedness of the mother has already been exposed. It is sad to realise that we have such people in our midst." In passing judgment, all the village headmen unanimously agreed that the mother had been wrong and that Kamuzunguzeni was not guilty.

Harry Chidoba Banda was present during the deliberations, from the beginning to the end, and ultimately, based on it, composed and sang a song, as follows:

"Kamuzunguzeni wazunguzga umoyo wa anyina.

Anyina bakamanya yayi kuti Kamuzunguzeni
wakaba kukhonde panyengo iyo iwo
anyina bakapangananga na chimbwe.

Achimbwe mwize kunyumba yane na usiku.
Kamuzunguzeni wagonenge
pabalaza, mwizakamurye, ndigho malipiro
ghanyanda yinu kuti mlandu umale."

("Kamuzuguzeni, has really troubled his mother.

His mother did not know that Kamunzunguzeni was around the corner when she was sealing a deal with hyena.

Hyena, come to my house at night,

24

Kamuzunguzeni will sleep in the living room, kill and eat him, as repayment for your *nyanda*.")

The lesson here is that whenever we want to reach an agreement with someone, the terms should not be as difficult as the condition agreed upon between hyena and Kamuzunguzeni's mother in this story, in which hyena ended up killing his friend out of ignorance. Hyena was simply trying to fulfil the promise earlier made to him. God intervened and made sure that it was the mother who had to pay for her cruelty. We should realize that each one of us has two important days in life: birthday and death day!

Chiduli cha mphangwe (literally a hill of vegetables) planted during the rainy season. (photo by author)

Chapter 5
Nyifwa ya Kalikwabo

Kalikwabo was a very clever lady, and she was also a thief. However, it was difficult for people to realise she was a thief since she was a trickster. A lot of the time people in her village used to complain that various items were being stolen, but they could not tell who was stealing the items.

One day, the village headman lost a whole pot full of beef relish (*dende la nyama*). The chief got furious and declared that the people should mount a thorough search until the thief was discovered. People did as instructed but to no avail. They reported back to the village headman who maintained his ground "look for the thief till you find him or her!" At this point, *banthu zeru zikabamalira* ("the people did not know what to do").

However, one person came up with an idea. Every person in the village was to go to the river where there was *chiziba chikuru na chakunjira chomene* ("a deep well with water inside"). The idea was each person, in turns, was to get immersed in the water and whoever stole the beef was going to drown. People agreed with this idea. Definitely, whoever did not steal was not going to drown. Before they started off for the river, one of them suggested finding out from the children from the households whether they ate beef relish the previous night. This was because usually kids told you the truth.

But even Kalikwabo's children vehemently refused: "Us, beef, when did we eat beef?" they responded in refuting the allegation. The time we ate beef, if we can remember correctly, was long time ago, during the rainy season. We remember vividly our mother telling us to go to sleep after we had finished eating since the house was leaking!" they emphasized. The people got impressed with the response and could not, therefore, associate Kalikwabo with the stolen beef.

They started off for the deep well (*chiziba chitali*), called *Dungulinya*. "Once we arrive each one of us should get into the well while the rest of us sing a song," they agreed. They were to sing the following song:

> *"Ninjani warya nyama ya fumu*
> *Dungulinya, telatela, eeh, mba*
> *Kalikwabo, Dungulinya, telatela!"*

> ("Who has stolen the chief's beef,
> *Dungulinya. Telatela*, eeh, is it
> Kalikwabo, *Dungulinya telatela*!")

(*Telatela* in this context is calling on the well to dry up if indeed the one inside is the one who stole the beef in question).

As they took their turns, it was noted that not one of them stole the beef since they came out clean. They could not drown in *Dungulinya*. *"Pamanyuma bakabona kuti Kalikwabo pakabavye pa banthu bose ba mu muzi wa fumu. Bakayamba kufumbana kuti kasi Kalikwabo wali nkhu? Zgoro likaba lakuti walikwabo. Bakati kamutoleni naye wazakapimike pa Dungulinya."* ("When everybody had taken his or her turn and the process was seemingly coming to an end, they discovered that Kalikwabo was not amidst the group. She was actually at her house, back in the village. "Where is Kalikwabo?" they enquired. "She is at her home," one replied. "Please, quickly go and bring her here, she too has to take her turn!" the group demanded.)

They brought her to the well and it was her turn to go into *Dungulinya* while the people sang in unison: "Who has stolen the chief's beef, *Dungulinya, telatela*, eeh, is it Kalikwabo, *Dungulinya, telatela*." After singing this song only once, the people noticed that Kalikwabo's legs started sinking into the water. At this point, they sang even more and more, repeatedly, and on top of their voices until Kalikwabo drowned completely. It, therefore, became clear that it was Kalikwabo who had stolen the chief's beef.

Upon interrogation, one of Kalikwabo's elder children explained that "indeed, we ate beef yesterday, but our mother took water in a pail, poured it to the roof of the house, upon which drops started coming to the floor." She thereafter told us to sleep "because it has started raining outside, hence the rain drops." People were stunned at Kalikwabo's crookedness. She was really a trickster.

The lesson from this *chidokoni* is that we should refrain from all kinds of crookedness because a day will come when all what we do will be exposed, just as it happened to Kalikwabo.

Chapter 6
Uheni wa Kaso na Chigolo

Long time ago there lived a couple who had a lot of livestock (*vibeto vinandi*). They reared a lot of chicken (*nkhuku*) and also stocked a lot of fish (*somba*). The nee-name for the wife was nyaVikosi. "*NyaVikosi wakaba munthu wa kaso, mukaka ndiposo wachigolo.*" ("She was a person who was very mean.") Early every morning, after opening *vitupa* (kraal for *nkhuku*), their chickens could fill the whole village, that is, literally every part of the village.

One day the husband told his wife, nyaVikosi, that they should kill one chicken for relish. However, nyaVikosi blatantly refused, saying "not now, let us do that when it is time to harvest millet." With this kind of response, the husband was let down since harvest period was far away. You may wish to know that this was happening when they had just sowed millet (seeds) in the gardens. In other words, several months had to pass before they could kill the chicken in question. Realising this, the husband came up with an alternative idea – to ask his wife to kill some fish instead. He was shocked to get almost the same response, as to the first chicken question - "not now, let us wait till it is time to harvest millet." Their conversation was in form of a song and it went as follows:

"*Chocholocho, chocholocho, chocholocho,
zalira malimba, zalira nkhuku*

*AnyaVikosi, anyaVikosi
tolanipo nkhuku tiryepo imwe,*

31

zalira malimba, zalira nkhuku.

Lero yayi, zalira malimba,
zalira nkhuku.
Lero yayi, zalira malimba,
zalira nkhuku.
Panyengo ya chithibu cha uchebele,
zalira malimba, zalira nkhuku."

("*Chocholocho, chocholocho, chocholocho,*
crowl *malimba*, crowl chicken.
AnyaVikosi, anyaVikosi,
may you kill one chicken for food?
crowl *malimba*, crowl chicken.

Not now, crowl *malimba*, crowl chicken (x2)
But during millet harvest and processing,
crowl *malimba*, crowl chicken.")

The husband was filled with pity and sadness seeing that his wife had maintained her ground on both requests. Thereafter, the husband cautioned his wife: *"AnyaVikosi, kaso ako muli nako, na ukaka ubo muli nabo ndiposo na chingolo icho muli nacho, vinthu vitatu ivi, nyengo yinyake vimuluziskeninge vyose ivi muli navo kwambula kuryapo nanga yingaba nkhuku yimoza panji somba yimoza."* ("One day your meanness will definitely land you in problems; you will lose everything, all your livestock, without tasting even one chicken or fish.") Despite this nyaVikosi maintained her ground "whether it is chicken or fish, let us simply wait for the millet harvest season."

You may wish to know that whenever they were "quarrelling" about whether to kill chicken or not (including

32

fish), both the chickens and the fish were listening and the question amongst them was "who will be first to be killed among us?" Both the chickens and the fish started living in fear because of this uncertainty.

One day the chickens started brainstorming: "How are we going to live since everyday (day in, day out) their song is "take and kill one chicken for relish?" They eventually agreed to approach one old male chicken (*gogo tambala*) for some wisdom as to how all the chickens would survive the ordeal. *Gogo tambala* responded: "since, we, chickens, we fail to fly for a long time, let us first of all get transformed (change) into *nkhwali* (wild guinea fowls). Once all of us do that, early one morning when they open our *chitupa* (kraal), we should fly away and never to be traced again." *Gogo tambala's* idea was warmly welcomed and, in a flash, they all changed into *nkhwali*. When nyaVikosi instructed her children to open chicken and let *nkhuku* feed, as they normally did, she was surprised to see all the chickens fly away into the bush until they could no longer be seen. Not even one chicken was interested to eat the grains in the compound. They flew away while "singing" *'kwali, kwali, kwali, kwali'*. The husband thereafter told his wife: "You have seen what has happened, all the chickens are gone. This is exactly what I have always been warning you."

When *somba* (fish) came to know about this development, they were filled with much more fear than before. They realised that they were the only available option during "quarrels" for relish between nyaVikosi and her husband. One fish told the others that they all had to recognize the fact that when it comes to relish, usually several fish were killed. And in this case, it was even more frightening as several fish would be killed on a particular day. They asked each other "is there anyone amongst us who is ready to be killed for relish?" Not even one was ready. Each and every fish wanted to live, as is the case with each and every creature.

One day they agreed to approach one of the eldest fish, *gogo somba*, for wisdom and the possible way forward. They were particularly looking for a survival strategy. *"Agogo somba, mwationa tabana binu tati pasi vuu, tamuchemani ndise kuti titoleko zelu."* (*"Gogo somba*, we, your humble children, have called on you to seek your advice as to how we may survive or prevent the tragedy that is to befall us," they reported their concern.) They continued, "as you are fully aware, *gogo somba*, this couple continues to sing a song, mentioning us in the process, as they quarrel over relish. The most frightening aspect is the realization that when it comes to fish relish, they have to kill a number of us at a time! Hence we are not only concerned, but afraid and filled with sadness that we will surely be wiped out." "What should we do, *gogo somba*, in order to survive?" they asked in unison, as if they had been rehearsing for days on end. "Is this the challenge that you have and is this the only reason you have sought my audience?" enquired *gogo somba*. "Yes, that is exactly our problem," they replied. "You have done well to approach me. Let me assure you that the solution to this problem is not hard to come by. By the way, it is you who have told me that because of the same threat and uncertainty, all the chickens have changed into guinea fowls, and have since flown away, not so?" asked *gogo somba*. "Indeed," they responded. "Okay, this is what we should do: once they give us food tomorrow morning, as they normally do, we should not go there. Instead, all of us should head for the lake and swim into deeper waters where they would not catch us, no matter what," advised *gogo somba*.

So, they all agreed with *gogo somba's* brilliant suggestion. Early the next day, when the couple opened the gateway to the feeding area, they were astounded to see all the fish escaping into the lake. NyaVikosi's husband confronted his wife: "Have you now seen that all our livestock have disappeared without us tasting even one of them?" NyaVikosi had no alternative option but to simply agree: "that is exactly what has happened." "I, personally, have realized that *ukaka* (meanness), and *chigolo* (selfishness) are very bad in as far as rearing livestock is concerned. We had a lot of livestock, chickens and fish, and now we have lost virtually everything," lamented nyaVikosi's husband.

The lesson to be learnt from this story is clear-cut: it is actually embedded in the repeated responses that nyaVikosi used to give her husband in reaction to his requests. *Ukaka* and *chigolo*, once followed in their entirety, may hinder someone from sharing whatever she or he has with others. The intention and feeling is as if he or she should only enjoy or benefit from *usambazi* (wealth) that they possess. In fact, in extreme cases, *ukaka* (meanness) would also deny even the owner from benefitting, for example, partaking in the eating of the slaughtered chicken. If it is clothes, such a person would not be ready even to wear his or her own clothes. In this case, of what benefits are such "possessions"? In most cases, such people end up losing everything, as we have noted from the story. That is why there is an old and enduring dictum on this which says *"ukavibona ryangapo, nyifwa yilije mazuba!"* ("When you have something, it is better to partake of it, for no one knows when he or she is going to die!") The old men coined this saying out of experience; they noted that such people end up leaving all their possessions behind upon death!

Chibaya cha mbuzi (traditional kraal for goats) (photo by author)

Chapter 7
Nyifwa ya Malenga Mwana wa Fumu

Malenga was a child with *nkharo yiheni* (bad behaviour). Whenever he crossed paths with his mother, he tended to use obscene words against her. He used to do this without leaving out any part of her mother's body: from head to toe. He had no regard for his mother. In fact, he used such obscene words against his mother as if it were any other creature, say, a wild animal. His mother always used to advise him that he needed to change this bad behaviour. At times, Malenga could confront his mother with such obscenity for no apparent reason. His mother used to warn him that such bad behaviour had the potential of landing him in problems: that once he did that to strangers, he could be severely beaten or even killed. As usual, Malenga could not take heed and could even challenge his mother, saying "nobody can kill me!"

One day Malenga and his friends, Kasiwa and Ngoza, went to the forest to collect *nkhowani* (mushrooms). As they were on their way to the forest, Malenga accidentally hit his leg into a tree stump (*chigodo*). At that point, Malenga started showering obscene words at the stump (*chigodo*): "You ugly stump (*wachigodo chiheni iwe*), you want me to be disabled when my mother gave birth to me without any disability!" He said all kinds of obscene words at the stump from roots to leaves. The tree stump never responded, remained quiet. If it were a person, Malenga could have been beaten right there.

Thereafter, Malenga and his friends proceeded to the forest and eventually collected *nkhowani* without any problems or hindrances. It was on their way back home that they saw

37

miracles (*minthondwe*). At the place where Malenga had said obscene words to the tree stump, they found that the *nthowa* (path) had been submerged by *phiri* (a hill) so that they could hardly pass through.

One of them, Kasiwa, told the others, Malenga and Ngoza, that he was going to knock at the *phiri* so that the latter could let him pass, saying "I was not the one who uttered obscene words at the tree stump." He lamented:

> *"Odi, abwana phiri, nilengeleni lusungu.*
> *Nijulileni, nisolote, nilute ine.*
> *Nkhamunenaninge ndine yayi,*
> *wakamunenaninge ni Malenga mwana wa fumu."*

("Hello boss *phiri*, have mercy on me.
Open the passage so that I pass through.
It wasn't me who was rude to you.
It was Malenga, the son of the chief.") x2

After he begged twice, the hill split into two, creating a passage in between, and Kasiwa passed through. Thereafter, the hill came back together.

Ngoza too begged the hill to create a passage for him to go through. He used the same words earlier used by Kasiwa:

> *"Odi, abwana phiri, nilengeleni lusungu.*
> *Nijulileni, nisolote, nilute ine.*
> *Nkhamunenaninge ndine yayi,*
> *wakamunenaninge ni Malenga mwana wa fumu."*

("Hello boss *phiri*, have mercy on me.

Open the passage so that I pass through.
It wasn't me who was rude to you.
It was Malenga, the son of the chief.") x2

The hill started splitting into two and, after begging the second time, the hill split into two; a passage was created and Ngoza passed through. Thereafter, the hill came back together, once again.

After noticing that his friends had passed through, Malenga too came closer to the hill. Before he even started knocking and begging, as his friends had done, the hill started squeezing him, and he was filled with fear, but he realized that it was him who had been rude to the tree stump earlier when they were on their way to collect *nkhowani*. Nevertheless, he too started begging the hill for mercy, saying:

"*Abwana phiri nigowokereni.*
Abwana phiri umu mukunifyenya ine nkhupulika kubaba
Abwana phiri, vikunitolera ku nyifwa ine
Abwana phiri nilengeleni lusungu, nijulileni, nisolote, nane nilute
Nkhamunenaninge ndine yayi
Wakamunenaninge ni Malenga mwana wa fumu."

("Hello boss *phiri*, please forgive me
Boss *phiri*, as you squeeze me I feel pain
Boss *phiri*, this takes me closer to my death
Boss *phiri*, have mercy on me, open the passage
So that I pass through, like my friends
It wasn't me who was rude to you
It was Malenga, the son of the chief.")

At this point, the hill asked him: "Who is Malenga?" Malenga responded, "it's me sir, but please forgive me," and he repeated begging the hill for mercy, as above. Despite this, the hill continued squeezing him, at the same time asking him "Who is Malenga?" until Malenga was sandwiched inside the hill. Malenga continued begging for mercy, but to no avail. In the end, Malenga got completely buried (enveloped) by the hill and this marked the end of his life.

Once they got back home, Ngoza and Kasiwa narrated everything to the parents: how on their way to the forest their friend, Malenga, bumped into *chigodo*; and how, thereafter, Malenga started showering obscene words at the innocent *chigodo*. They also narrated *minthondwe* that they came across on their way back home after collecting *nkhowani*: how the path had been submerged under the hill. They went on to explain that the two of them (Ngoza and Kasiwa) managed to beg the hill for a passage, telling the hill that it was not them, but Malenga, the son of the chief, who had been rude; that thereafter the hill split into two and they passed through.

They further explained that they doubted if Malenga, too, would manage to pass through, because if he had done so he too would have reached home since time had elapsed since this happened. The parents demanded that Ngoza and Kasiwa should take them to the scene where this had happened.

When they reached the miracle place, they realised that both the hill and Malenga were not there. But they found that a tree with beautiful flowers had grown at the site. At that point Malenga's mother started crying saying "Malenga's stubbornness had led to his death; I always advised him to change his behaviour, but he could not listen. I always told him to stop using obscene language." The mother continued to explain that she even told Malenga, her son, that one day such obscene words would be directed at wrong people and this could lead to his death. "Look what has happened, exactly what I said," the mother continued. "If he had changed his behaviour, he could have been alive today," complained the mother.

The lesson in this short story is that children need to get instructions and advice from their parents. If parents say this is wrong; stop doing wrong things, children need to obey. Otherwise, fate awaits them, like Malenga, who even after dying, his body could not be buried since it simply went missing.

The children need to know that even in the Bible it was written "respect your mother and father so that the days of your life should be numerous in this world."

Chapter 8
Nyakamwilo Wataya Mwana Wake

Long time ago there lived a woman whose name was nyaKamwilo. One day she went hoeing in her garden. As she was hoeing, there came a man named Solo from behind the hills. They then greeted each other quite well. NyaKamwilo asked the stranger: "Who are you?" The man replied: "My name is Solo." (Solo is locally the name of a bird.) Thereafter, Solo asked nyaKamwilo to lend him her child temporarily saying *"mama, unibwelekeko mwana wako nkhachezgepo naye, namuwela naye."* ("Lady, would you allow me to take your child, chat with him and I will bring him back later.")

NyaKamwilo agreed to allow Solo take away her child. *"Wakabonga kuti walimepo makora pa munda chifukwa Solo panyengo iyo wakatola ntchito ya ulezi wa mwana."* ("In fact, she was grateful as it allowed her to concentrate on farming without disturbance from the child.") After Solo went away with the child, the mother continued with farming, undisturbed, until she got tired.

Around eleven o'clock in the morning, nyaKamwilo was tired and decided to go back home. However, she could not start off since Solo was not yet back with the child. Consequently, she decided to continue with farming while waiting for Solo to return.

After some time nyaKamwilo was so tired that she stopped hoeing and sat under a tree, waiting for Solo. With time she noted that the sun was about to set but Solo was nowhere to be seen. She was filled with grief and sorrow. She regretted: *"Nimanyenge kuti ndimo a Solo bayendelenge mphanyi*

43

nanguzomela yayi kuti balute namwana wane." ("Only if I had known that Solo would take this long before bringing back my child, I would not have allowed him to go way with my child.") At this moment she remembered a *ChiTumbuka* proverb: *"walagha waliwa,"* which simply means that at that time there was nothing else she could have done other than wait for Solo to return.

Solo did not come back and this time the sun had just set. She then started singing a sad song calling upon Solo to come back with the child. It went like this:

> *"Solo, Solo zaunipe mwana wane*
> *Mayilele, mayilele, dazi latchona.*
> *Solo pakwiza kumunda nanguba*
> *namwana, nanthembe, nangubo, najembe*
> *mayilele, mayilele dazi latchona.*
> *Solo palanawela kwambula mwana,*
> *nthembe, ngubo najembe*
> *namuyowoyachi kukaya a Solo imwe?*
> *Mayilele, mayilele, dazi latchona."*

("Solo, Solo come back with the child
mayilele, mayilele, the sun is set
Solo, when coming to the garden
I was with the child, feeding bottle, wrapper and a hoe,
mayilele, mayilele, the sun is set
Solo, if I go back home without my child,
what will I tell the people at home?
Mayilele, mayilele, the sun is set.")

NyaKamwilo noted that Solo was not coming back. She then sang the song loudly for the second time (repeating the song as above). When she turned and looked towards Hola Mountain, she spotted Solo coming back with the child on his back. "I am back, I am back," Solo said. NyaKamwilo then started drying her tears after realizing that her child was back. "Why take so long?" she asked. "I am very sorry for the delay," replied Solo. "Although I have taken too long, don't worry, I have taken good care of your child. In fact, he is not hungry at all," continued Solo. "Just look at the honey all over his mouth. Consequently, you will not bother to breast-feed or give him porridge," added Solo.

NyaKamwilo then took the child, put him on her back, ready to go home. At that point, Solo requested that he should be allowed the following day to take the child away again, as he had done. After noticing that Solo had taken good care of the child (had even fed the child), the mother agreed to the proposal.

The next day, Solo came and took away the child. However, after hoeing a long time, nyaKamwilo realized that Solo was nowhere to be seen with the child until sunset. The mother was filled with grief again. She started calling upon Solo to return with the child with the same song as before:

"Solo, Solo zaunipe mwana wane
Mayilele, mayilele, dazi latchona.
Solo pakwiza kumunda nanguba
namwana, nanthembe, nangubo, najembe
mayilele, mayilele dazi latchona.
Solo palanawela kwambula mwana,
nthembe, ngubo najembe
namuyowoyachi kukaya a Solo imwe?

45

Mayilele, mayilele, dasi latchona."

("Solo, Solo come back with the child
mayilele, mayilele, the sun is set
Solo, when coming to the garden
I was with the child, feeding bottle, wrapper and a
hoe,
mayilele, mayilele, the sun set
Solo, If I go back home without my child,
what will I tell the people at home?
Mayilele, mayilele, the sun is set.")

Even after singing loudly, she noted that Solo was nowhere in sight. The people at home eventually heard the loud, sad singing from the direction of the maize gardens. Some of them noted that the voice was similar to that of nyaKamwilo. A short while later they noticed that, indeed, it was nyaKamwilo who was arriving home, looking very gloomy. "What has happened now that you are coming home 'empty-handed': no child, and with his feeding bottle?" people asked her.

NyaKamwilo narrated the whole story: how Solo had 'borrowed' the child to chat with him as she was working in the garden, and how he promised to return the child later in the day. She reported that, in fact, this was the second day. She explained that on the first day Solo had done the same and, though later, he had returned the child after sunset. But, on this second day Solo had not returned with the child. Out of curiosity, the people then asked nyaKamwilo where Solo was from. "I don't know," she replied. The People cried out loud, telling her that Solo had no permanent home: *"Solo nimayingayinga walije muzi wachikhazi chenecho."* ("Solo is a wanderer and has no permanent home of residence").

"Dazi linyakhe wangaba mu phiri la Hola, linyakhe mu phiri la Solola, Perekezi, Zumwanda, panji Chiring'oma. Yula ntchito yake njakupenja njuchi mumapiri. Mapiri agho wakwendamo nganandi chomene."

("One day he (Solo) would be in Hola Mountain, the next day in Solola, then Perekezi, Zumwanda, or Chiring'oma. Solo's job day by day is looking for honey in the mountains.")

At the point, the people told nyaKamwilo that she had lost her child on her own volition by letting a total stranger, someone without a permanent home, take him away. They further told her that it would not only be difficult, but also futile to start looking for Solo, knowing pretty well that the latter had no notable home. "If we try to look for him in Hola Mountain, he may be in Solola. When we go to Solola, he will have left for a totally different place, hence the difficulty and futility of looking for him," they emphasized. They told nyaKamwilo that even reporting the matter to the police was equally futile because the basic thing is that we do not know where Solo comes from. In fact, "where is Solo from?" is the basic question that we will come across from the police. Consequently, even the police will not know where to start from in looking for Solo.

The lesson from this story is that as people we need to be careful whenever we want to lend out our property. The first thing that we need to know is the details of someone who wants to borrow things from us: their name, surname and home village. In addition, it is not good to rush to accommodate a stranger in your home, arguing *"mlendo nijumi namachero wakuluta"* ("a visitor is more like morning dew, which easily dries up"). Some people rush to accommodate such visitors, especially when we have a lot of belongings and wish to be kind and share our wealth. It is, however, easy for visitors to steal such property and disappear at night. In such a case, as has been seen from this story, it would be futile to report such a case to the police because of lack of personal details about the thief in question.

Munda wa vingoma na ntchunga (a maize and beans garden) (photo by author)

Chapter 9
Ubwezi wa Somba na Munkhwere

Long time ago there lived *Somba* (fish) and *Munkhwere* (monkey) and the two became intimate friends, in line with a *Tumbuka* proverb which says *"kanda apa nane nikandepo"* (i.e. close relationship). It is worth noting that the two had been friends for fourteen solid years. *Somba* came from the lake while *Munkhwere* originated from the mountains adjacent to this lake.

Whenever *Somba* came to the mountains for a visit, he came using a boat and brought along a lot of foodstuffs, for example, different types of small fish (*usipa*): *"wamululi na wakuphika"* (sun–dried and boiled) including good and delicious types of fish, for example, *nkholokolo*. *Munkhwere* and his relatives used to warmly welcome *Somba*, their dear friend. After staying for some time, *Somba* would say bye and head back home. At this point, *Munkhwere* would organize foodstuffs for his friend: the kind of foodstuffs that are hardly found at the lake i.e. different types of natural fruits: *"mphampha zakusubilathu zinandi, vikuyu mabere, mbula na masuku."* Upon arrival at the lake (home), *Somba* and his relatives used to have a nice time since this was the only time they could eat rare mountain food, for instance, they used to prepare special, delicious relish out of *mphampha* (*"Mphampha bakazitolanga nakuphika dende ngeti ni vimbamba"*).

Their friendship had no problem whatsoever. People from both sides (mountains and the lake) used to benefit from this friendship in various ways: *Munkhwere* used to share gifts with his mountain people, such as various types of fish brought in by *Somba* from the lake; on the other hand, *Somba* too used to share with his lake people various foodstuffs brought by *Munkhwere* from the mountains. People from the two sides did not think that this intimate friendship would come to an end.

After some time, *Somba's* father fell sick. The son (*Somba*) took him to different medical practitioners (doctors), both traditional doctors (herbalists) and western medical doctors to no avail. In fact, the condition was deteriorating with time. One day *Somba* met *ng'anga yachifipa* (traditional doctor) who told him that he knew the cause of the sickness (disease) and that, furthermore, he knew its treatment. However, the healer complained about the lack of *chizimba* (one of the ingredients needed for the medication). *Somba* asked the *ng'anga* about the type of *chizimba* that was needed for the medication in question. "The heart of *Munkhwere*," the healer replied and continued as follows: *"kutola mutima ndopa zichali fefefe!"* ("getting the heart in question while it is still bleeding!")

Realizing that there were no monkeys at the lake, his home area, *Somba* filled by Satan's deceit, devised a plan of getting the heart of his dear friend, *Munkhwere*, by calling him over to his place immediately. He came up with a trick, a way of getting *Munkhwere* into his carefully-crafted trap, as follows:

"Abwezi mwizakuno kunyanja maulendo ghanandi chomene, kweni mukuwerera waka pano pakaya; kose kula kwati chee nyanja njakutchona pachoko kweni kula mudima wati biribiri njakutchona chomeme sono imwe abwezi kula mungakenda makora yayi pakuti mwabanyithu mundazgowere kwenda mumaji. Pala mungati mutima lipu mbwenu mwabila. Sono chiwemi chomene nchakuti pala tikuluta imwe mutima winu tizakauleke pano pakaya. Paulendo uwu mwamuona vinthu vyakupambana-pambana. Kumazele tendamuonanga ba chigwele naba mung'ona.

Ndipo pakati apa ghakwenda ma wato tendamujumphananga na somba zamitundu ya kupambana-pambana, zikwenda mumizere nge mba silikali bankhondo!"

("My friend (referring to *Mukhwere*), you have been coming to the lake, visiting us, for a long time but you don't visit places; your visit only ends here at home; (pointing) you see there, where there are red rays, the lake is shallow; but where it is green, the lake is very deep, hence with you, you can't be comfortable there since you are not used to swimming. Since you can easily drown in such deep waters, the best arrangement is that whenever we will be going to such deep places, we should make sure we leave behind (here at home) your heart. Let me assure you that on this journey you will have the privilege of seeing different water creatures: for instance, on the left side of the lake we will see hippos and crocodiles, and at the centre where boats and canoes usually pass, we will be passing through different varieties of fish, swimming in straight lines as if they are soldiers marching unto war!")

It is worth noting that before meeting *Somba,* his friend, *Munkhwere* was lucky to bump into a good Samaritan who confided in him all the plans of *Somba*: to get hold of his heart while blood was still oozing and hand it over to the *ng'anga* as *chizimba* for medication of *Somba's* sick father. *Munkhwere* was advised to devise his own way of saving his life in the event that his friend, *Somba*, starts suggesting that they should leave *Munkhwere's* heart back home. The Samaritan impressed on *Munkhwere* not to disclose this to *Somba* as that would be jeopardising the Samaritan's life since *Somba* would definitely kill him.

At this juncture, *Munkhwere* made a solemn promise (to the Samaritan) not to reveal this to *Somba*. They later parted. Later on, *Munkhwere* was invited by *Somba* and the latter briefed him on their planned visit to the lake (as earlier narrated in the story). When the appointed day came, *Somba* told his friend that "today is the day we are visiting the lake, as I had told you." *Munkhwere* replied: "I am totally in agreement with your proposed visit to the lake. In fact, I was filled with enthusiasm and curiosity when you first proposed this to me; it would really make a difference rather than what I normally do - not going beyond your house whenever I am visiting!" However, he went on to explain to *Somba* that there was a little problem:

> *"Kweni pali suzgo wa mubwezi wane. Suzgo ndakuti ise tabamunkhwere usange tayenda ulendo utali ngati ni umunkwizira kuno kunyanja, mitima yithu tikwenda nayo yayi. Ntheura umu ine nilili kuno kunyanja mutima wane uli mukhuni kunyumba kumapiri. Usange ukukhumba kuti tikatole chiri kwa iwe."*

("There is a small problem. The problem is that whenever we, monkeys, embark on a long journey, for instance, from the mountains to the lake (here), we don't move with our hearts; hence as I am here my heart is right at home in a tree. It is actually up to you whether we should go back home to get it or not.")

At this point looking at the gravity of the matter in hand *Somba* had no choice but to agree to go to *Munkhwere's* home (in the mountains) to get the heart. Just after embarking on his home-ward journey, the condition of *Somba's* father deteriorated. The parents tried phoning him back, but they could not get through. The lake was also rough that day. Before *Somba* and his friend *Munkwere* reached Usisya, *Somba's* father passed away. The parents at home were filled with grief since *Somba* was far away when this happened.

Because of the uncertainty surrounding his return from the mountains and realising that his father had been sick for a very long time, the parents and relatives at home held a caucus on the way forward during which they agreed to go ahead and conduct the burial ceremony in his absence. So, indeed, his father was buried next to where *Somba's* grandfather, Mr. Zumwanda, had been buried.

While this was happening at home, *Somba* and his long-time friend were in the midst of a heated disagreement:

> *"Munkhwere wakakwela mukhuni lake*
> *mupaka kukaneng'aneng'a, nakwamba*
> *kuchema a Somba mwachimwazga:*
> *A Somba, a Somba imwe. He! Imwe na*
> *ine ubwezi wamala!"*

("*Munkhwere* climbed his tree up to the tip
of it and started calling upon *Somba*
sarcastically: *Somba*, let me tell you one
thing; our friendship is over!")

Upon hearing this, *Somba* replied
"What do you mean our friendship is over?

Our friendship started long time ago and
we have been very close all this while.
Furthermore, you climb the tree to its tip
and you start pouring your sarcasm on
me; is this supposed to be bad omen?
Let me tell you that when we left home (for
this place) my father was seriously sick."

At that point, *Munkhwere* seemingly added salt to injury:

"Yes, you think I don't know, that's why you were
looking for my fresh heart (with blood still oozing)
so that you hand it over to the *sing'anga* (healer)
as *chizimba*."

Somba replied angrily: "Who told you such blatant lies?
Could I do such a thing? All these are lies!" *Somba* yelled.
"Whatever, but let me tell you that I am not coming down
there: whether you spend the whole day waiting for me to
come down this tree," charged *Munkhwere*. In fact, your
continued stay (waiting) there is at your own peril. And very
soon it is hunger which is going to deal with you down there;
and I am not releasing any fruit for you from this tree,"
warned *Munkwere*.

Somba, at this juncture, complained bitterly as to who had
told his friend *Munkhwere* about the heart secret. "I wish I
knew this person, I would surely kill him or her," fumed
Somba. He knew for sure that his friend, *Munkhwere*, was
determined and there was no way he was going to change his
stand. He concluded from his friend *Munkhwere's* behaviour
that something was definitely wrong at home (bad omen). In
fact, he suspected that this foretold doom at home, that is,

death and burial of his very sick father! He was now determined to embark on his homeward journey, not having any stop-overs along the way as is usually the case.

Upon arrival at home, he was welcomed by his home people, quite alright. After normal greeting the people asked: "Where is your friend, *Munkhwere?*" He says he is not coming with me," replied *Somba*. "Why? Have you two quarrelled?" queried the people. "No, only that there is someone here who told him (*Munkhwere*) about the plan we had of getting his heart for purposes of *chizimba* to prepare *mankhwala* for my sick father," explained *Somba*. At this point, one of the elders shouted:

> *"Bakoleni a Somba, bakoleni a Somba. Iwe*
> *wamunung'una wabo bakoleni a Somba. Kasi*
> *mukukhumba kuti agogo binu bamuphalire za*
> *nyifwa munyinu uku wali chakuyimilira? Bakoleni*
> *a Somba. Enya khalani pasi."*

> ("Can you assist *Somba* to formally sit down.
> Hey you (pointing/referring to his younger brother)
> assist your brother, *Somba*, to sit down. Do you
> want your grandfather to break the sad news to
> *Somba* before he formally sits down? May you
> (*Somba*) sit down first.")

Thereafter, *Somba's* grandfather narrated the whole story about his father's death just after *Somba* had left for *Munkhwere's* home.

> *"Mwana wane Somba nagogo wako nilije*
> *chakuti ningayowoya chazeru. Zeru*

55

zilikumalira papo juzi. Mukuti waka wato
kwele, mundayende mutunda utali,
kuno mbwenu matenda gha awuso
ghasinthirathu. Banyako kuyezga kuchita
telephone nokukola yayi. Nyanja
nayo ukani. Ine nakale nindayiwonepo.
Mundafike ku Usiska kuno awuso mbwenu
bakutileka waka. Kuona kuti munyane
wakalwara nyengo yitali, nakuti wafwa
zimbambo zili yowata, tikakhala pasi banja
lithu lose,ndipo nyifwa tilikubika mayilo kopa
kuti munyithu wavundile pachanya."

("My grandson, *Somba*, I don't have anything
sensible to tell you. When you had just left for
Munkhwere's place (home), before you even
covered any noticeable distance, your
father's condition deteriorated. Your friends
tried to phone you, but to no avail. Before
you even reached Usisya your father passed
away. Realizing that he had been sick for
a long time and that he had lost a lot of weight,
we had to sit down and discuss as a family on
the way forward, during which we agreed to
proceed with the burial, though in your absence.
So, indeed, burial was yesterday to prevent the
(dead) body decomposing as a result of delay.")

However, the only painful thing (they continued to tell
Somba) is that you have lost two things at a time: You have
lost your father and also friendship with *Munkhwere*, the kind

of friendship which even we, your parents, were benefiting from.

"Phepani mwana wane pakuti vilikuyoboyeka kale na balala kuti 'pala maji ghathika kuti ghakuyoleka yayi'. Kweni pala mukwenda mu ng'anga ndipo ng'anga yikuti munkhwala wake chizimba chake nimutima wa munthu ngati ni iyo yikatenge chizimba nimutima wa Munkhwere, kukhwaskanga kuvibalo vya munthu mungayilondezganga yayi chifukwa ng'anga zantheula zipasuzi."

("We are very sorry for what has happened, however, there is literally nothing that we can do since there is an old saying that 'you can't cry over spilt milk'. However, whenever you visit traditional healers and the medical prescriptions are involving human body parts, as in this scenario, do not follow such prescriptions since such healers are simply divisive.")

They went on to condole and console him by advising him (*Somba*) to take heart following the death of his father. They told him to leave everything in the hands of God, the omnipotent and omnipresent. They also told him that they had buried his father next to where they had buried his grandfather, late Mr. Zumwanda. "Tomorrow we will take you there so that you see your father's grave, as tradition demands," they promised him.

Nyanja (lake): home of *somba* (fish) (photo by author)

Chapter 10
Kusoba kwa Maji

Long time ago there was a year when water had been very scarce; in fact, even wild animals could hardly find water to drink. However, there was one well which had water. It is worth noting that there lived a harsh, vicious wild bird at this well, which used to chase all the other animals away, stinging them in the process, claiming ownership of the well. The bird in question was too possessive and thought the intruding animals would end up drying up its well. This development put all the other animals in an awkward situation. However, for lack of an alternative, the animals could still go to this well and face the wrath of this bird.

As this problem continued unabated, the animals agreed to be going one by one, one after another, to fight this vicious bird with the hope that once it was killed, they would freely be partaking in the water at this well. The first animal to go to confront the bird was *Njati* (buffalo). The other animals warned it to be careful otherwise it would end up being killed by this bird. *Njati* was boastful and explained the approach it would take in confronting the vicious bird:

"Chakudankha namuchipenkhera mamphina ndipo pala chikwiza kufupi namuchigwaza na zimphondo zane. Chamuona, chingakanitonda yayi."

("Firstly, I am going to "spread" mucus on it, and if it continues advancing, I will finish it with my horns. Verily, verily, I promise you, the bird will not withstand this.")

59

At that point, all the animals agreed that *Njati* should be the first to go. During the confrontation, *Njati* tried spreading mucus at the bird, as planned, but to no avail. The bird charged at *Njati* and started stinging it. At that point, *Njati* resorted to using its horns, again it did not work. After realizing that it could not withstand the fight, *Njati* had no alternative but to run away.

Upon arrival, all the other animals noted that *Njati* came back running and were curious to find out how the encounter had been. *"Nawerako nakuti nalumika chomene, ndipo ningayakoso yayi, pala ni nyota njachi yinikome,"* replied *Njati*. ("I am back and I should report that bird stung me heavily; in fact, I have no intention of going back, if it is thirst I am ready to die of it.") Upon hearing this, *Zovu* (elephant) volunteered to go after *Njati*: *"Lekani sono nilute ndine, pala chikwiza kwaine namuchikola na chitamba chane nakuchidyaka na malundi ghane ngakulu kuluska mwanyane mose."* (Let me go after *Njati*; and when the bird approaches me I am going to grab it using my *chitamba* and thereafter I am going to stamp on it using my feet which are larger that all of you.") The other animals agreed saying "go and let us see how strong you are." Just upon arrival at the well, the bird charged at *Zovu*, stinging and "scratching" using its crawls. *Zovu* tried all its tactics, including trying to stamp on the bird, but everything failed. The more *Zovu* tried this and that, the more it got attacked more and more by the bird. Eventually, *Zovu*, too, ran away.

From a distance, the other animals saw blood all over *Zovu* and after finding out how the fight had gone, *Zovu* succinctly replied: "I will not go back; in fact, I am now in great pain!" When the other animals noted that *Zovu*, the largest animal of all, had vowed not to go back again, they were bewildered; they did not know what else to do and who else to try. They were surprised to see *Fulu* (tortoise) volunteering to go after *Zovu*.

All the other animals broke into laughter: *"A Fulu yamuyeghani ni nyifwa, mwamuchimbira uli na mendelo ghinu ghakukwakwatuka?"* ("This may be the influence of death upon your life: come to think of it, how are you going to run away at the heat of things with your slow pace?" queried the animals.) *Fulu* replied: *"niphakeni phula linandi pa musana wane wose."* ("Can you apply glue all over my back!") They did as requested but they had no hope whatsoever that *Fulu* could emerge victorious. At that point, they let him go. He started off.

Upon arrival at the stream, the bird asked: "Are you sure, *Fulu*, it is you who has come to fight me?" *Fulu* confirmed that, indeed, he had come for a fight. The bird reported, sarcastically: *"A Fulu muli kwakatu – kwakwatu kuti mulwenge nkhondo na ine. Imwe mwangulibona pakufuma dazi pakunjila mulibonenge yayi; muhanya uno imwe yinu ni nyifwa."* ("*Fulu*, are you serious you want to fight me when you can only crawl, failing to walk properly. Let me assure you that you were lucky today to see the sun rising and you will not see its setting because you are going to die!") *Fulu* replied majestically: *"wakufwa wakumanyikwa yayi."* ("You can't tell who is going to die during a fight.") He was saying this with his head outside his shell, fuming with anger, ready for confrontation.

In no time the fight had begun; the bird charged at *Fulu*:

"Chiyuni chikamulotokera Fulu. Fulu wakwiza mutu wake mubachi lake njizge. Chiyuni chikuti lekani nikaswe musana. Bati pamusana go basanga mulomo wawila. Lekani nichidyake, basanga lundi lawila. Badyakeso nalinyake basanga nalo lawila.

61

Mbwenu nkhongono zabamalila, kwati mapapindo phu-phu-phu;
pamusana wa Fulu vwaba."

("The Bird charged at *Fulu*. In reaction, *Fulu* simply
hid his head inside his shell. The Bird then decided to hit
Fulu's back using the beak. Upon doing that, lo, the beak
got stuck! Then it decided to strike using one leg; the leg
also got stuck. In trying to strike using the only remaining
leg, the Bird was surprised to see that the second leg got
stuck too. Thereafter, the Bird lost all the remaining
energy and simply "collapsed" at *Fulu's* back.")

Realizing that the Bird was completely trapped on his
back, he got his head out of his shell and started off for the
other animals with Bird on his back.

When approaching home, the other animals noted that
something dark was approaching them. At this point, "hell
broke loose," animals wept:

"Nyama zikachiluka nakuyamba kulira kuti a Fulu chinthu
chakoma abonani chikwiza kuno. Nyama zikayamba kuchimbila
kubopa kuti nazo zingakomeka nga ni Fulu. Zovu yikati lekani
nane niti waka lupiri zwe chingiza kakoma ine mayilo
chikanipweteka. Vinyama vikapulika mazgo ghakuti 'lekani
kuchimbila ndine Fulu; chiyuni chila chikatisuzganga chawila
mulomo, malundi ghose na mapapindo bubo'."

("*Fulu* is no more! See the beast is heading towards
us. All the animals fled away afraid of being the next
victim. Even elephant could not brace the situation and
had to run for safety; he still had fond memories of the
merciless attack the previous day. Then the animals heard

Fulu's voice 'don't run away, it is me, *Fulu*, the bird that has been wreaking havoc is the one trapped, bar and all, on my back!'")

The animals then recognized *Fulu's* voice and stopped running away. Then they gathered at one place.

"Fulu wakafika nacho pafupi vimaso vili chee! Banyake bakati lekani sono tichikome; kweni muchikome makora mungapweteka munyithu. Bakachitinya ku singo uku bakuchitataula pamusana wa Fulu. Bakumala kuchitataula mbwenu nacho chafwa kale. Zovu yikapempha vinyama vinyake nabukali chomene chifukwa yikaba yichali kupulika ulwilwi umo chikayiluma. Ndipo bakayizgomerezga kuti yichitekete namalundi; Zovu yikayesa kuvinapo ngeti nigule wa chitivili mupaka dongo pela bii!"

("*Fulu* then approached the other animals with the Bird on his back, with its eyes having turn red! The other animals then decided 'let us now kill it!' and yet while everyone agreed, others advised to exercise care, not to hurt *Fulu* in the process. They strangled the Bird while physically 'extracting' it from *Fulu's* back. When they finished doing this, the Bird had already died. However, *Zovu*, still not contented, begged the others to let him 'deal with the bird', since he could still feel the pain from the previous day's fight. All the animals agreed with his request to tramp on it with his feet; and what *Zovu* did was more of 'dancing' on it till there was nothing left; the Bird had been ground to dust!")

At this juncture, all the animals celebrated that the Bird had been killed. The birds started singing *"nyimbo yamagubo"* as follows:

> *"Kayuni Karyarya kawila mulomo,*
> *kawila, niti go kawila mulomo*
> *kawila, niti dya, kawila mulomo*
> *kawila, niti dya, kawila mulomo*
> *kawila. Phu-phu-phu kawila*
> *mulomo, kawila."*

("The clever Bird got stuck its beak,
got stuck, *"go,"* got stuck its beak
got stuck, *"dya,"* got stuck its beak
got stuck, *"dya,"* got stuck its beak
got stuck, *"phu-phu-phu,"* got stuck
its beak, got stuck!")

After they were through with their *"mugubo"* dance, they asked each other as who their leader was going to be; the one who was going to look after the well. They all shouted *"Fulu!"* *Zovu* who was king of all the wild animals declared that no other animal apart from *Fulu* would be allowed to go around with a shell since he had freed them from bondage i.e. from the water crisis. This is the reason why it is only *Fulu* of all the wild animals who goes around with a shell (*bachi*).

The lesson from this story is that we should refrain from underrating each other based on, say, one's stature, saying "what can that one do." What we need to know is that each and every person has his or her own unique talent when it comes to doing things. In this story, we see *Fulu*, a very small animal, being the one who grabbed a very vicious Bird which could not allow other wild animals partake in water from a well it claimed to be its own possession!

Chapter 11
Uheni wa Mitala

Long time ago there lived a man who had two wives and these wives gave birth to daughters (one each) almost at the same time. These children grew up together. The husband (of the two wives) had gone to Harare (Zimbabwe) to take up paid employment. He left his wives and the children behind at home.

The two daughters were close friends; and they were always together (doing everything together). However, the first wife (*mwanakazi mulala*) hated this: she did not want the two to be fond of each other like this. On the contrary, the second wife (*mwanakazi muchoko*) had no grudge against *mwanakazi mulala*, her friend (*munyake*). Unfortunately, *mwanakazi muchoko* died while the husband was at work. *Mwanakazi mulala* took advantage of this development and displayed hatred towards her late friend's daughter.

Despite this, the daughters continued to love each other. The remaining mother started to ill-treat *mwana wa malemu* (the daughter of the departed mother); almost to the point of not feeding her. One day the mother sent the two to draw water from the stream (*ku dambo*). She gave an old perforated tin to *mwana mulanda* (the orphaned child) and a good tin to her (direct) daughter. When the two arrived at the stream, the one with a good tin quickly drew water and returned home in no time at all. The opposite was true with her friend:

"Wakayezga kuteka maji kweni pala wathwika ghakasululanga. Wakathiramo mchenga kuti maji ghaleke kusulula. Wakafika kukaya mwakuchedwa chomene uku maji

ghali sulululu thupi lose. Wakadandaula chamumtima, nakukumbuka banyina, wakati 'amama babenge bamoyo mphanyi suzgo lose ili kulije'."

("She tried to draw water, but whenever she put the tin on her head, the water got lost through holes. As a solution, she put sand inside the tin to block the holes. As a result of this struggle, she reached home very late, still with water splashing all over her body. She grieved in her heart saying 'if only my mother were alive, all this could not be happening'.")

What *mama wamoyo* (the surviving mother) actually wanted was to find means of killing the orphaned daughter without anyone noticing; not even her step sister. She devised a strategy of sending the two daughters to draw water from the stream. This time she took *chithini chakudoloka* (an old perforated tin) and gave it to her direct daughter; and gave *chithini chiwemi* (a good tin) to *mwana mulanda* (the orphaned child); the aim was to ensure that they should arrive home separately and at different times.

While the children were at the stream, she dug *chikhululu chitali chomene* (a deep pit) and inside it lit the fire on which she cooked beans with the aim of sending *mwana mulanda* inside to re-light the fire, knowing pretty well that this time *mwana mulanda* would be the first to return. Her plan was to bury her alive once she is inside the pit. This is exactly what she did. At this point no one, not even her daughter could suspect that her friend had been buried inside the pit.

When her daughter returned from the stream, she asked her mother, while water was equally splashing all over her body, about the whereabouts of her step-sister. "She has gone playing where you usually play, go after her you will find her," her mother replied. So she went looking for her. Unfortunately, she checked in all the usual places and did not find her. She later reported this to her mother: that she did not find her. The mother replied, advising her of what to do next: *"Kapenjenge waka kwenekuko"* ("Just go and continue looking for her there").

At this point, the daughter was filled with grief and sadness and she started singing a very sad song:

> *"wamunyane uli nkhuni iwe, adada bawela bayegha katundu, katundu ni salu, yinyake nja iwe yinyake njane."*

("Where are you my friend, our father is back and has brought back *katundu* (goods), *katundu* in the form of *chitenje* (wrapper); one is for you and another is for me.")

The step sister, buried inside the pit, heard her friend crying in grief and she replied, saying:

> *"Namanya ine lero kuti anyoko mbafwiti, banijimila pasi pachanya baphikapo nchunga."*

("I have realized today that your mother is a witch; she has buried me in this pit and is cooking beans on top of this pit.")

Upon hearing this, the step-sister was confused, realizing that the response was coming from below the surface at her mother's verandah. Coincidentally, within a short period of time, their father actually returned home. "Where is your friend?" the father asked her. "I have brought you goods (*katundu*), e.g. wrapper (*salu*), one is for you and the other one is for her," continued her father. This is what she responded:

> "*Adada lekani nimuyowoyelenipo ivo vikachitika na amama. Amama bakakhumbanga yayi kuti ine nendelenge lumoza na munyane. Ndipo amama badoko bakati bafwa, vinthu vikasuzgirathu, pafufi Wini kuti bamunole chakurya. Ine vikanikondweskanga yayi.*"

("Father, let me share with you what has been happening. My mother did not like me going around with my step-sister. After the death of my step-mother, the situation deteriorated, to the extent of *Wini* almost sleeping on an empty stomach. To be quite candid, I didn't like what was happening.")

She further went on to narrate to her father the scenario leading to the disappearance of her friend. "My mother a couple of days ago sent us to draw water from the stream. She gave me a good tin while gave my friend an old, perforated tin for the exercise. After drawing water, I quickly reached home since I was using a nice tin, whereas my friend took longer as she was struggling to mend the tin; she came home with water all over her body."

She later on narrated the scenario which had actually led to *Wini's* disappearance two days before.

"On this day, mother also sent the two of us to draw water again from the same stream. This time, mother gave me an old tin, while she gave my friend a good tin. She left me behind, obviously, since my tin was old and perforated and I was, therefore, struggling to stop the leakage (using sand).

Upon arrival back home, I asked mother about my friend's whereabouts. Mother responded saying: "go where you always play and you will find her there."

She then continued by telling her father that after this she went out to look for her friend, but to no avail. "When I tried to probe further, mother only responded saying 'continue looking for her, you will surely find her'. At this point, I was filled with sadness and grief. I then resorted to calling upon her, loudly, while singing, saying "Where are you my friend? Our father is back with goods (*katundu*), and has brought *salu* for you and me." At this point, I was surprised to get a response that 'she knew that our mother is a witch, that she buried her inside a pit, covered the pit with soil and on top of it cooked beans'. You may wish to know that the voice was coming from below the ground behind my mother's house."

Her father asked her "if you can ask your step-sister 'Where are you?' Can she respond?" "Yes," she replied. Then she went ahead asking her friend:

"Wamunyane uli nkhuni iwe, adada bawela bayegha katundu, katundu ni salu, yinyake nja iwe yinyake njane."

("Where are you my friend, our father is back and has brought back *katundu* (goods), goods in the form of *chitenje* (wrapper); one is for you and another for me.")

Just after this, the step-sister responded from below the ground:

"Namanya ine lero kuti anyoko mbafwiti, banijimila pasi, pachanya baphikapo nchunga."

("I have realized today that your mother is a witch; she has buried me in this pit and is cooking beans on top of this pit.")

At this juncture, the father cried loudly; thereafter he dug from where the voice was coming. He found the daughter in a deep pit, with long hair. He got her; cut her hair, and later bathed her with soap. Thereafter, he called his wife and asked her: "Is this how cruel and crude you can be, just because your friend passed away?" The wife had no response. The husband got very angry and beat her up until she bled, from the nose and other areas. In fact, this marked the end of their marriage.

The lesson from this story is that when people are in a polygamous family, they are not supposed to vent their anger on innocent children as a result of the challenges they face in the family. Innocent children do not deserve such ill-treatment, as narrated in this story. Why? Simply because they are not a cause for the problems in question: they are innocent. In this story, it was good to let the children continue loving each other, as we have seen, despite the fact that one of them lost her mother.

Chapter 12
Sanje za a Chakurya Nkhumunda

Long time ago there lived a man who was a great farmer (*chikumbe*) and he used to have a lot of farm produce throughout the year. During the rainy season (*nyengo yazinja*) a lot of people used to go to him for piecemeal jobs (*maganyu*). This man was very good in that he used to treat his workers with kindness by, for example, giving them good pay. In this way most people liked him. These people, however, in sharp contrast, always faced food shortages in their households. Whenever this farmer noted poor crops in people's gardens, he knew for sure that more and more would eventually approach him for *maganyu*.

Gradually, whenever he was chatting with his friends, he used to say sarcastically that *"chakurya nkhumunda"* (food is in the garden); implying that whenever there is poor yield then this means hunger in a household. People started noticing that he was gradually becoming boastful and stubborn: that he was the only great farmer in their village.

Because of his insistence that *"chakurya mkhumunda"* (food is in the garden); people gave him the name *Chakurya Nkhumunda*. Eventually he started accepting this name because it implied that people were recognizing him as a lead farmer in this village since nobody equalled him. He was always talking about farming and even the village headmen started calling him by his new name.

People in this village realized that they were spending a lot of time doing *maganyu* in the gardens of *Chakurya Nkhumunda* at the expense of working in their own gardens. One year they, therefore, agreed as a group to work very hard in their gardens in order to produce enough yield to avoid working for *Chakurya Nkhumunda*. At this point, *Chakurya Nkhumunda* got worried that if people were indeed going to have enough food, then this would spell doom for him as he would face critical labour shortages, most of his gardens would not be attended to as a result of this development. He was, therefore, worried that his scale of production would drastically go down.

Consequently, this implanted hatred in him fearing that there would be many farmers like him in this village. He, therefore, resorted to witchcraft: he developed *nyanga* (fetishes).

> *"Wakapanga kasupa kamankhwala ndipo (mkati) wakawikamo kamunthu. Kamunthu aka wakakaphalira kuti pala banthu bati waka lute mu minda yabo iko kayimbenge nyimbo kukaya kuti pala banthu bapulika bazizwenge kuti ninjani wakuyimba kukaya tiyeni tikamubone."*

("He made a 'fetish' object (*nyanga*) and inside it he put an imaginary small person. He instructed this small person that whenever people just arrived in their maize gardens, it should start singing (loudly) at home so that when people listen to the singing they should be surprised as to what is happening, in the process abandoning their gardening and heading back home to check.")

This is how the singing went: *"Mba mbaliwatimba watimba n'goma timba. Timbani ng'oma tibazibanizge minda yigone palikomila kale palikomila."* ("Beat the drum, let us disturb them from gardening, moreover the soil is dry and cannot be worked.")

Whenever the drum was beaten, everybody abandoned gardening and went home to see who was beating the drum, but when they reached home, they never spotted anyone. But when they checked on their wrist watches they realized time had gone, and they concluded that they would go back to the gardens the next day since it was already late. But what they did not know is that whenever this was happening *Chakurya Nkhumunda* was not coming home; he was busy working in his garden. This continued for a long time, indeed.

But eventually people noted that the problem was escalating, and they agreed to lie in waiting in order to catch the one who was doing this. They chose four energetic men who lay in waiting. They, thereafter, as a group went to their respective gardens arguing 'this small person cannot disturb our gardening'. Just upon arrival in their gardens, the person started singing as usual: *"Mba mbaliwatimba, watimba ng'oma timba. Timbani ng'oma tibazibanizge minda yigone pali komila kale palikomila."*

Those men who had laid in waiting drew closer and closer and eventually surrounded him and managed to grab him. When they tried to check what they caught, they realized they had grabbed the *supa* (fetish). *"Kasi iwe ndiwe ukwimba kuno kukaya mwakuti ta banthu titondekenge kulima makora?"* ("So it is you who usually beats a drum whenever we have just arrived in our gardens?") At this point, the *supa* agreed that indeed it was him who was responsible for the singing. However, it clarified that it was doing this following the request from *Chakurya Nkhumunda*; that it was the latter who had instructed him to do so.

The intention by *Chakurya Nkhumunda* was to disturb people in their gardens so that they should realize poor harvests (yield) so that they should continue doing *maganyu* in his gardens. The people later on confronted *supa*: "If we ask *Chakurya Nkhumunda*, is he going to accept that indeed it is him who sent you?" *Supa* agreed without hesitation. They, thereafter, summoned him and indeed he accepted that, in fact, *supa* was his possession. He went on to clarify that he did all that to ensure there was no other great farmer in the area. If this happened, he was assured that all people would contribute working in his gardens, especially during lean months (*myezi ya njala*).

At this point, people concluded that although *Chakurya Nkhumunda* had for a long time presented himself as a good and kind man, full of benevolence, but this time he had showed himself to be selfish and jealous. And the village headman said that with the behaviour he had displayed, in the process trying to disturb development in the area, the punishment was death sentence, but because for a long time he had been good to people in the village, and because it was a first offence, he had been forgiven. However, the village headman declared that his *supa* was to be destroyed there and then. Chakurya Nkhumunda obliged. They then called *Musaope*, a man who had the courage to destroy things associated with evil spirits (*masenga*). He was instructed to bring a hammer with which to destroy the *supa*. Upon crashing the *supa* with hammer, there came a voice "ayo!" from the *supa*, but the people urged *Musaope* to completely destroy it.

We should learn from this story that it is good to be a great farmer like *Chakurya Nkhumunda*, but we should attain this status through upright and normal procedures, unlike the approach that *Chakurya Nkhumunda* followed: trying to suppress others through evil means so that he, alone, should be well-to-do in the village. This was actually against development in the area. Instead, let people prosper through their hard work. Let us avoid being jealous and selfish. If people work hard be it in crop farming or livestock farming, let them prosper. In the end, all this is for the general good of the entire village and the household members within it. For instance, with good yields, there is no hunger for every household throughout the year.

Chapter 13
Selina na Basungwana Banyake

Long time ago there lived a girl named Selina. She had seven female friends and together with her they totalled eight. They were all at school. There girls were in classes five to seven. Everything was going on well at school. With time these girls came of age and young men (*majaha*) started approaching them for marriage proposals. Even their parents were on the forefront advising these girls on the need to get married.

All the other seven girls eventually got married informally, that is, without formal weddings. However, Selina refused, arguing she had to complete her studies first. While in marriage, her friends had children; others one child, others two children; while others even three.

With time people started laughing at Selina; saying she was not going to get married. What interested parents was the fact that they could easily have grand children through early marriages. In fact, after some time even Selina's mother joined the band wagon: laughing at her that she had overstayed before getting married. The intention was to influence her to get married. However, Selina maintained her ground; she had to complete school first.

During this time, Selina had no friends to chat with. She started going around alone, for example, when going to draw water, to fetch firewood and when going to school. One day, there was no firewood at her mother's place and off she went to fetch firewood.

While fetching firewood in the forest, Selina heard a voice calling: "Selina, Selina, I am here, your friend." Upon hearing this, she looked around, but did not see anybody. She then continued fetching firewood, but she heard the same voice: "Selina, Selina, my mother, I am here." When Selina tried to look around, she saw a big snake (*sato*) having surrounded her. She was filled with fear. She thought for a moment and realized it was not advisable to throw away firewood since there was literally nothing at her mother's home. At the same time she could not run quickly with firewood on her head. She then decided to jump across the snake and ran for dear life, going towards her home. To her surprise, the snake also immediately ran after her: "I will not leave you," the snake shouted.

Despite this, Selina decided not to throw away *mtolo wa nkhuni* (a bundle of firewood) on her head: "If it is the work of the devil that I be devoured by this snake today, let it be so!" she retorted. "But with God's power and guidance, the God that created both people and snakes, I will reach home," she continued.

Upon reaching home, she threw away the bundle of firewood and ran quickly towards her *nthanganeni* (small hut) for hiding. Just as she tried to open the door, before she entered her house, she noticed the snake was right behind her. Upon entry and as she tried to close the door behind her, she noticed that the snake too had already entered. At this point, Selina ran out of ideas. She did not know what to do.

She could not report the matter to her parents for fear of being reprimanded that it's because of her dilly-dallying that now she had a snake as a suitor! (*"Kuti wabayoboyele bapapi bake wakatondeka chifukwa wakabopanga kuti bamunenenge kuti ni ving'unu vyake ndivyo vyamutoreska chisato kuthengele kuti chibe chijaha chake."*) In fact, it was going to be very strange; the first of its kind; for a snake to be one's suitor.

Within a short period of time, Selina was surprised to hear the snake telling her to boil water for it to bathe. "Make sure the water is too hot," clarified the snake. At this point, Selina had no alternative, but to oblige. Once ready, she brought very hot water to the snake. The snake advised her to stay firm by holding onto the pillar of the house (*mzati wa nyumba*). The snake then advised her to pour all the hot water on it. Selina thought "this is my relief as the snake is surely going to die."

Upon pouring the hot water on it, Selina was filled with shock and surprise to see that the snake gradually started getting transformed (i.e. metamorphosis) and, lo, immediately after Selina saw a white man sitting on a chair! "Get all the snake skins (*vikonkhomoliro*) and throw them into a deep pit, and cover it with tree leaves," Selina was advised.

Selina was still afraid to report all these developments to her parents. Obviously, the question could have been: "Where is the white man from?" since Selina's friends and cousins saw no-one entering her *nthanganeni*. There was this practice that whenever *majaha* (suitors) arrived in the village, they were first being met by the in-laws and cousins whose interest was to assess the visitors' behaviour or conduct, their dressing and their general outlook and appearance. Once they were not impressed, they then told the potential suitors that all the ladies in the compound had already accepted marriage proposals by other suitors. And that, in fact, even *malobolo* (bride price) had already been settled and that they were only waiting for the official wedding to officially hand them over to their husbands. But if they were impressed, then they invited the ladies to take their potential suitors (*majaha*) into their *nthanganeni* for courtship and proposals to begin.

While she was busy making sense of all what had happened, Selina heard the white man saying: "Selina, let's go." Selina then asked: *"Kasi mulayilenge yayi ku bapapi bane?"* ("Are you not going to say bye to my parents?") The white man responded: *"Bapapi bako bangazomela yayi kuti nilute nawe chifukwa bapapi bane bandalowolepo kanthu."* ("It's not advisable for me to do that because your parents would not accept since my parents have not paid the bride price.") The white man continued: *"Ine nkhunena kuti tilutenge na iwe pa nthengwa ya chisomphola."* ("I want us to get married informally.") At that point Selina thought in her heart: "Let me go with this white man since people in this village scorn me that I will never get married."

While on the way, the white man kept on singing: *"Selina tilutenge banthu bakulindirira kukaya."* ("Selina, let's go home, people are waiting for us.") Upon arrival, the white man introduced Selina to his parents: "This is Selina my wife; we got married informally. I got her from where I stay." His parents were filled with joy that their son was back after a long time and, in addition, that he had brought home *mukamwana* (a daughter in-law).

Selina discovered that almost everything one would need was there in the village: maize mills, grocery shops, piped water, and brick and iron-roofed houses with electricity. At this point, she decided to wait and see the behaviour and general conduct of her white husband; that if he was bad mannered, then she would leave for her home village. As she stayed on, she realised that both her husband and parents were good mannered: she never complained of anything at her house.

However, she only had one concern: that her husband should oblige that they should both go to see her parents, who for a long time did not know her whereabouts. Her husband obliged but told Selina to wait a bit. Later Selina gave birth to a baby girl. After three months, Selina started pressing her husband again – that they should visit their parents since her husband's parents never sent any message to Selina's parents that she had been married.

At last, the husband agreed to Selina's demand. They started off in a beautiful car. They carried along a lot of goods (*katundu wakupambanapambana*). They also put on nice suits with spectacles on. Upon arrival, people were surprised to see a car parked at the house of Selina's mother. Upon closer look, they realised it was Selina with a baby on her back and that she was in the company of a white man. At this point the whole village was filled with joy and they celebrated that Selina was still alive. To express joy and happiness, they slaughtered *ng'ombe yituba* (a white cow) for Selina and her husband.

After staying three days, they went back home where Selina's husband told his parents how well they had been received. Later on they paid *malobolo* (bride price) and it was a happy family; in fact, much more than the families of Selina's seven friends who got married much earlier.

This story tells us that it is good for parents to encourage children to complete their education before getting married. After school, it is when daughters find good educated husbands, including white men (*bazungu*), similar to what had happened to Selina. When we say:

"*mwana watengwa kwa muzungu kuti tikunena mzungu wachikumba chituba yayi. Kweni ku munthu wamasambilo ghawemi uyo wawoneseskenge kuti iyo namuwoli wake babe na nyumba yiwemi, baryenge makora, bavwalenge makora, ndipo pala bali na bana babatumenge kusukulu ziwemi kuti nabo basangenge masambilo ghawemi."*

("our daughter is married to a white man, we do not mean a man with a white skin, rather we mean a well-educated man; a man who will ensure that he, together with his wife, will have a decent house, good food, descent clothing, and if they have children they will be in a position to send their children to good schools where the children will attain the much-needed education for a good future.")

Selina and her husband devised a programme to be visiting Selina's parents once a year. And whenever they visited, people in the whole village were filled with envy, saying: "Selina's mother is no longer our friend in this village," what they meant here is that Selina's mother never lacked anything at her house because of gifts. At this point, most people in the village came to realize that it was bad to allow daughters to get married before completing their education.

Ukwati (wedding ceremony): *bapapi* (parents) need to encourage *bana basungwana* (daughters) to get married after attaining education (*masambiro*) (photo by author)

Chapter 14
Nkharo ya a Mujima

There lived a man whose name was *Mujima*. He had a wife. *Mujima* used to drink beer a lot and he had a habit of coming back home late at night. While drunk, he used to come home singing:

> *"Ine ndine Mujima wazangala.*
> *Ndine wazangala*
> *nkhufuma kumagule gha usiku wazangala*
> *ndine wazangala."*

("I am *Mujima wazangala*
I am *wazangala*
I am coming from night dances, *wazangala*
I am *wazangala*.")

He used to put on *"mangenjeza"* (anklets) around his legs and while walking they (*mangenjeza*) used to produce sound *"ngenje-ngenje."* Whenever he was about to reach his house, he used to shout on top of his voice, notifying his wife about his arrival:

> *"Aboli bane ndine Mujima nafika.*
> *Pulikani mangenjeza ghane agho*
> *ghali ngenje-ngenje*
> *Ine nafuma kumagule gha usiku."*

("My wife, I am *Mujima*, I am back.
Listen to the sound of *mangenjeza*
ngenje-ngenje.

87

I am coming from night dances.")

At that point, the wife used to open the door for him, but upon checking time she could notice that it was very late at night – at dawn. The wife used to advise her husband to stop coming home late and that when coming home, to stop making noise, to be coming home quietly for fear of being attacked by thugs and criminals (*vigebenga*). Apart from that, *vigebenga* would know that while away at night, the wife was alone in the house, and they would attack her one day. Despite this advice, *Mujima* never changed.

The wife tried to advise the husband to be coming home early from the so-called night dances, but to no avail. Eventually, the wife started getting suspicious about such night dances, thinking that there was an element of witchcraft (*ufwiti*). The wife simply became tolerant; otherwise she could have called it quits.

With time *chimbwe* (hyena) knew that almost each and every night *Mujima* was away from his home. Hyena, therefore, decided that he too would go and knock at *Mujima's* house. This is what Hyena said:

> *"Ine ndine Mujima wazangala*
> *ndine wazangala*
> *Nkhufuma ku magule gha usiku wazangala*
> *ndine wazangala."*

("I am *Mujima wazangala*
I am *wazangala*
I am coming from night dances, *wazangala*
I am *wazangala*.")

"My wife, it's me your husband, I am back; open the door," hyena said. But since the wife mastered *Mujima's* voice, she did not open the door. *"Chimbwe wakaluta uku dozo liri rya-rya-rya. Wakaghanaghana za kuti walute ku ng'anga kuti yikamovwireko zelu iyo wangendapo kuti aboli ba Mujima bakajureko kuti wakabarye."* ("Hyena went away almost salivating, having missed his delicacy (Mujima's wife) by a whisker. Hyena then decided to consult the *sing'anga* (witchdoctor) on how to implement his plan.")

After *chimbwe* briefed the *sing'anga* on how *Mujima's* wife utterly refused to open the door, the *sing'anga* asked *chimbwe*: *"Kasi iwe wukimba mazgo wuli?"* (Which voice did you use when singing your song?") *Chimbwe* replied *"nkhayimbanga kwakuyana na mazgo ghane gha uchimbwe."* ("I was singing using hyena's usual voice.") The *sing'anga* told hyena that as long as he used hyena's voice, he could never succeed in his plans of killing *Mujima's* wife. The sing'anga quizzed *chimbwe* further: *"pala ukatenge apulika mangenjeza ghane agho ghali ngenje-ngenje, iwe ukavwala mangenjeza?"* ("When you were telling *Mujima's* wife saying listen to the sound of *mangenjeza*, did you actually have *mangenjeza* on your legs?"). In addition, when singing, make sure you go and emulate Mr. *Mujima's* actual voice. "Once you follow these instructions, you will surely succeed," the *sing'anga* assured hyena.

Later *chimbwe* bought *mangenjeza*, put them on his legs, and also emulated *Mujima's* voice. He then went to *Mujima's* house at night and sang the song exactly as *Mujima* used to do when coming home from his night dances: "I am *Mujima wazangala*, I am *wazangala*. It's me *Mujima*, I am coming form night dances. Just listen to the sound of my *mangenjeza 'ngenje-ngenje'.*" *Mujima's* wife then opened the door and she was devoured by *chimbwe*.

The lesson from this story is that whenever we go, be it for beer drinking, or night dances, as was the case with *Mujima*, let us come back home earlier, but also without making noise, that is, quietly. What *Mujima* used to do is an attraction to dangerous criminals (*vigebenga*) at night.

Chapter 15
Mwanakazi Muchoko Wakabila pa Chingwe pa Kazuni

Long time ago, there lived a man who had three wives. He was very good at preparing traps (*misampha*) for various types of animals including birds. One day, he caught *nkhanga* (guinea fowl) and gave it to the youngest (third) wife to prepare for cooking. He later went to the bush to continue with his job of setting traps (*kuthya misampha*).

While in the forest, he had all the hope that once back home the third wife would bring him *sima*, with cooked *nkhanga* as relish. But alas, he was surprised to get *sima*, with *ntchunga* (beans) as relish. The husband asked: "haven't you prepared *nkhanga*?" The wife replied:

> *"Nkhanga nanguphika kweni apo ine nanguluta kudambo kuti nkhateke maji, bana munyumba bangulekamo mwazi ntheura nchebe zangunjila munyumba nakurya dende lose mupaka zaswa namuphika wuwo."*

("I indeed prepared *nkhanga*, but when I went to draw water from the river, the children left the door open and as a result dogs entered the house and ate all the relish I prepared. In fact, they have even broken the clay pot.")

The husband got very angry and said *"uyo warya nkhanga yane, warya nthubaluba"* ("the one who has eaten my *nkhanga*, he or she has eaten *nthubaluba*"). The husband continued probing, asking the wife to be very frank if she had been the one who ate the relish in question. He insisted that it would be very wrong if she was the one and was simply using dogs as a scapegoat. However, the wife maintained her ground and refused. At this point, the husband became furious and repeated saying "the one who ate the relish (*nkhanga*), he or she had eaten *nthubaluba*."

The husband extended the message to all the three wives saying he was going to discover the one who ate *nkhanga* at whatever cost. They all then decided to put a rope (*chingwe*) from one end of Lake Kazuni to the other end. The arrangement was that all the three wives, including 'the dogs which the third wife said had eaten the relish had to cross the lake using this *chingwe*. This was a trap to catch the thief (*munkhungu*). The husband said anyone who did not eat the relish would cross, but the one who had eaten the relish was going to drown.

The husband started singing his song, saying:

"*nkhanga yane, nkhanga yane, amama uyo warya nkhanga yane warya nthubaluba.*"

("My *nkhanga*, my *nkhanga*, the one who has eaten my *nkhanga*, has actually eaten *nthubaluba*.")

When the process started, behold all the dogs crossed the lake using *chingwe*. He then continued singing the song above. Thereafter, the first (eldest) wife easily crossed over. Later it was the turn for the second wife, who equally crossed over with ease. Lastly, it was the turn of the third (youngest) wife. During this time, the husband continued singing. But behold, when she reached the middle of the lake, the rope started shaking (*kundengendela*). The third wife cried uncontrollably and asked the people to rescue her, as she was going to drown. She then opened up:

> "*Nkhanga nkharya ndine, nkhabisanga nkhaopanga a fumu bane kuti banganitchaya.*"

("I was the one who ate *nkhanga*. I was concealing, afraid of being beaten by my husband.")

Then all the people shouted: "You have eaten *nthubaluba*!" The rope continued shaking (*kundengendela*) until she drowned at last.

All the people, including the husband concluded that what had caused her death was her canning behaviour, arguing that if she had accepted that it was her who had eaten *nkhanga*, then definitely the husband would not have given such a heavy sentence – death.

As such, as people, we need to refrain from such behaviour. Whether you have done something wrong, but once you are confronted, it is good to own up and not deny. Once you accept, this action in itself would lessen the anger of *"mwenecho wa chinthu icho chanangika"* ("the owner of something which has been affected"). In this story, *"nthubaluba ni mazgo gha nthembo kuti uyo wakarya nkhanga mpaka wafwe, ngeti ni umo mama wakabilira pa chingwe pa Nyanja ya Kazuni"*) ("*nthubaluba*" are swearing words calling for the death of whoever ate *nkhanga*, as was the case with the third wife who got drowned as she was trying to cross Lake Kazuni using *chingwe*").

Chapter 16
Munthu uyo Wakapanda Nyungu za Vipindi

Long time ago there lived a man who grew special pumpkin seeds locally called *nyungu za vipindi*. The pumpkin seeds (*nyungu*) grew healthy and produced a lot of fruits called *vipindi*. The farmer was a very happy man because of this development. He chose one fruit (*chipindi*) of the many fruits (*vipindi*) and paid special attention to it. In fact, he used to care for this *chipindi* more than other *vipindi* (fruits):

> *"Wakachiphamaskanga uku na uku na kuchilongola umo chingabila za muwukulu na kuchilongolaso umo chingabila za muwutali. Chipindi chikaba chikulu na chitali chomene."*

("While this *chipindi* was not fully ripe, he used to "mould" it to be both big and elongated. In fact, eventually it became too big and too long.")

The owner eventually started singing a song for this *chipindi*, as follows:

> *"Ine ndine jungu, yawa jungu tale, yawa jungu. Munibone pa kwenda, yawa jungu tale, yawa jungu. Nkhuyesa kuthunduzuka, yawa jungu tale, yawa jungu. Thunduzu, thunduzu, thunduzu, thunduzu, yawa jungu."*

("I am *jungu, yawa jungu tale, yawa jungu*. Look at how I walk, *yawa jungu tale, yawa jungu*. I am actually 'jumpy' when walking (*kuthunduzuka pakwenda), yawa jungu tale, yawa jungu. Thunduzu, thunduzu, thunduzu, thunduzu, yawa jungu.*")

This *chipindi* kept on growing and people started getting surprised. They even started wondering as to what was inside, since it started being 'jumpy' when walking (*kuthunduzuka pakwenda*). It could not walk properly. Some people started suspecting that this *chipindi* contained bulky *katundu* (goods) inside.

Later on the people decided to break this *chipindi* to see what was inside. Upon breaking it, they discovered people inside and a lot of money. Then the people asked each other: "who was going to be the owner of those people?" The response was that these people belonged to the village chief (headman), who had the authority and responsibility over the people in his village. "What about the money?" "Who was the owner of the money?"

At this point the chief immediately stood up:

"Ndalama nazo zibenge zane chifukwa munthu uyu wakapanda nyungu za vipindi ni munthu wane, ndipo charo ichi pali munda nacho nchane. Ndiposo nyungu izo wakapanda nazo mbuto yake yikasangika muno mucharo chane."

("Even the money will be mine because the farmer who grew pumpkins which produced this *chipindi* is mine, even the piece of land on which pumpkins grew is mine. What is more, the seeds that were planted were found in my area.")

People realized the chief was very selfish and not considerate since he wanted to control and own everything –

goods (*katundu*) and money that came out of this *chipindi*. People tried to reason with the chief saying that the money should rightfully belong to the farmer, but to no avail. On the other hand, the people thought that the people who had come out of the *chipindi* belonged to the chief. They believed it was his duty to find and distribute land to them.

When the chief maintained his stand, the farmer concluded that he could no longer continue staying in this village. As such, he secured a piece of land from another chief. With time, more and more people left for other villages since they became demoralized. In the end, *"ufumu wabo ukabwanganduka"* ("his chieftaincy crumbled") since all the people left.

The lesson from this *chidokoni* (story) is that chiefs need to be self-less and considerate when dealing with their people. The people from the *chipindi* rightly belonged to the chief since it was his duty to look after their welfare, for example, provision of farming and settlement land.

> *"Ndalama yikenela kuba phande la mulimi. Ntheura mulimi ndiyo nthena wakatolapo ndalama nakubapako. Pala bakaona kuti wakhala chete mphanyi bakamupempha kuti wabapeko, kuluska kuyesa kutanila katundu yose."*

("The money was supposed to belong to the farmer. As such, it should have been the farmer, himself, giving the chief part of this money. If the chief noted that the farmer did nothing, it was right and proper for him to ask for some money, rather than selfishly claiming all the money and *katundu* from the *chipindi*?.")

Chapter 17
Mama Walayila Mwana Wake

There lived a mother who had two children: the older child was *Roma* and the younger one was *Bayenkhu*. *Roma* used to stay in *Malambo* (Zambia) while *Bayenkhu* continued to stay with her mother. However, their mother was sickly; "*amama bawo bakalwaranga kabiri-babiri*" ("she used to fall sick now and again"). The mother knew in her heart that there was a sickness that never completely left her. She did take medication, but she hardly noticed any real improvement. It is such sickness that usually takes one to an early grave. "Now if I die with whom is *Bayenkhu* going to stay? It is, therefore, important that I tell her that once I die, she should go to her sister who stays in *Malambo*," she thought.

This mother grew a lot of millet (*lipoko*) in the garden (*munda*). But her health condition continued to deteriorate. She started telling *Bayenkhu* this through a song:

"Fya mbalame, kachenjelekete, kachenjelekete.
Pala nafwa ine, kachenjelekete, kachenjelekete
ulute ku mukulu wako Roma wakukhala
ku Malambo, kachenjelekete, kachenjelekete.

Fya chavuba, kachenjelekete, kachenjelekete.
Chavuba lipoko, kachenjelekete, kachenjelekete."

("Fly away birds, *kachenjelekete, kachenjelekete.*
When I die, *kachenjelekete, kachenjelekete.*
Go to your sister, *Roma*, who stays

99

in *Malambo* (Zambia), *kachenjelekete, kachenjelekete.*")

Noting that the birds were 'destroying' the *lipoko* farm, the mother decided to call *Roma* and her husband (from *Malambo*) to assist *Bayenkhu* scaring away the birds at their farm since *Bayenkhu* was still young: the task of scaring away these birds was too huge for her. *Roma* and her husband came. However, they only stayed one week before their mother passed away. People advised *Roma* to continue scaring away birds in order to safeguard the remaining *lipoko*. In addition, they told *Roma* that she was now *Bayenkhu's* 'mother' following the death of their mother. They advised her to take good care of *Bayenkhu*, just like their mother used to do.

Before the public, *Roma* agreed to do as requested: to continue looking after the *lipoko* farm and taking care of *Bayenkhu*. But after the burial ceremony (*chivumbi*), *Roma* started sending *Bayenkhu* to scare away the birds alone at the farm. When she was away, *Roma* and her husband used to eat *sima* with nice relish (*dende*), for example meat or well-cooked beans. When *Bayenkhu* was back, they used to give her *sima* with *mpholozi* ("worms") as relish. While she had not eaten anything, but noting that *mpholozi* was the relish, she used to say I am enough (*nakhuta*). And *Roma* used to warn *Bayenkhu* that she was surely going to die if she continued refusing to eat. *"Bunganyadanga ngeti nimula bukanyadilanga pala amama bakaba bamoyo yayi, ine nikhumbenge kunisuzga-suzga yayi."* ("Do not give me problems by being choosy food-wise, the way you used to do when our mother was still alive"). As a result, *Bayenkhu* never led a happy life as before. *"Wakakhalanga khuma-khuma ngeti ni nkhuku yakuzumbwa."* ("She used to lead a lonely life as if it was a wet chicken.")

One day, *Bayenkhu* deliberately delayed in returning from the *lipoko* farm, hence *Roma* asked herself: "Why is *Bayenkhu* so late in coming back from the farm today?" She then decided to follow her up. While on the way, she met two eagles (*nombo*) which attacked and wounded her ("*nombo zikamupala chomene*") as if it was punishment for ill-treating her younger sister, *Bayenkhu*.

The lesson from the story is that if our parents have died and left behind, in our care, siblings, we should not ill-treat these siblings the way *Roma* used to do with her younger sister, *Bayenkhu*, for instance, by giving her *sima* with *mpholozi* as relish.

Chapter 18
A Zumwanda Bafwa Chifukwa cha Soni

Long time ago, there lived a man whose name was *Zumwanda*. This man was a big farmer and whenever there was *njala* (food shortage), *"banthu bakaponeranga kwa iyo"* ("all the people in the area got relief from him"). Most people used to do *maganyu* (piecemeal jobs) for him. He used to grow almost everything – maize (*vingoma*), cassava (*vikhabu*), sweet potatoes (*mboholi*), pumpkins (*majungu*), and millet (*lipoko*).

People in the area used to like him since he used to pay very well. He never boasted that "without me, hunger was going to wipe them out." Because of his kind-heartedness, his farming (*uchikumbe*) used to go on well; for a very long time, that is, for so many years.

Unexpectedly, there came great hunger (*njala yikulu chomeme*), the kind of *njala* that even great farmers (*vikumbe vikulu*) did not have enough food in their households. This is what the wife told her husband, *Zumwanda*:

> *"A Zumwanda nase tiyeni tikalimiskengeko tuvikhabu kubanyithu abo baliko na tuminda twa vikhabu. Abonani sono libenge zuba la chitatu tikugona na njala ndipo mukubona kuti njara iyi yayamba kukoma banthu. Lekani kuchita soni."*

("Mr. *Zumwanda*, let us also swallow our pride and do some *maganyu* in the farms of those who still have some cassava. Look, it's now three days we are sleeping on empty stomachs. And you can see that this *njala* has already started killing some people. Let us not feel shy and ashamed.")

However, this is what *Zumwanda* responded:

"I have been a great farmer (*chikumbe*) for so many years and this is the first time for us to be hunger-struck, as a result I can never do piecemeal jobs for someone else's farm."

Then the wife advised: "If that is the case, then go and beg for some food, cassava (*tuvikhabu*) from your relatives who at least have some cassava." Mr. *Zumwanda* replied: "those who have some cassava are by far very young in comparison to me, so that I am not supposed to beg food from them." However, the wife insisted, saying "It does not matter whether you are old to them, if you do not do so, we will surely lose some of our children due to this *njala*. Look, we have already started burying children who are dying of *njala* in the neighbouring villages," the wife continued, pumping sense into her husband. However, Mr. *Zumwanda* maintained his ground: "I cannot stoop so low as to beg from those who are young to me."

The wife continued to persuade him to go and beg a little something from the relatives: "Whether they give you very little cassava, it will still make a difference. In case, they, too, don't have something, but you will have tried, at least." *Zumwanda* continued to refuse both begging and doing *maganyu*. At this point, his wife asked: "Now that you refuse to beg and do some *maganyu*, how are we going to take care of our children?"

Mr. *Zumwanda*, in response, devised a plan:

"Ine nifwenge kafwadala, pala nafwa mubaphalire banthu kuti a Zumwanda bafwa. Nangauli kuli njala yikulu, kweni banthu ba muzi withu uno bakuyezeska kusonkha vyakurya pa nyifwa. Ine bunimanyiskenge kuti sono babuka namwe kuluta ku malalo kuti bakabike. Pala bali pafupi na dindi ine namusukunika mu bokosi. Ndipo banthu bamuzizwa. Bamuthula bokosi nakulijula, banunisanga kuti tumaso tuli nda! Ntheura bamukuti Zumwanda yangumukomola ni njala ndipo bamukuti muphikileni tubala wamwe. Pala namwa tubala ine namukhizgila dala mutima pasi. Bamukuti wasisimuka, tiyeni tiwelenge nayo ngwa moyo."

("I will pretend to have died, and when I 'die', you will tell people that Mr. *Zumwanda* has died. Although there is heavy hunger, the people in this village try their best to make contributions during funerals, especially food stuffs. You will inform me when they start off for burial. When they are very close to the grave, I will shake inside the coffin and the people will be shocked. They will then put down the coffin, open it and, behold, they will find me with my eyes wide open! They will, then, conclude that Mr. *Zumwanda* did not actually die, but had simply passed out as a result of hunger, and they will prepare porridge for me. Upon taking porridge, I will there and then regain my strength. They will, then, prove that I am fully alive and we will head back home.")

After all this happened and they were eventually back to *Zumwanda's* house the chief declared that everyone should return to their home so that all the food which had been collected for the funeral should now only be utilised by members of *Zumwanda's* household. When people had retired to their homes, *Zumwanda* asked his wife: "Have you seen now that we have managed to secure the scarce food?" The wife agreed. They started eating the food, but, alas, in the end the food ran out.

Then the wife asked her husband: "now all the food that people contributed is gone, what are we going to do?" *Zumwanda* replied: "I will pretend to have died again. This time tell the people that *Zumwanda* has really passed away." People were later told that Mr. *Zumwanda* has really died this time around. A lot of people said: "we knew *Zumwanda* would not live long since he last stayed in the coffin for a long time and he only regained his consciousness very late in the afternoon when *bazukulu* (those responsible for burying the dead) were about to start the burial process."

When the chief heard that *Zumwanda* had actually died, he ordered his people to contribute foodstuffs knowing that relatives would come from far and wide to be present when burying their relative, *Zumwanda*. People, once again, made handsome contributions.

When time came to take *Zumwanda's* body for burial, his wife started calling upon him: *"A Zumwanda bukani abonani banyamula bokosi bamumubikani wamoyo."* ("Mr. *Zumwanda*, please wake up, look they have carried your coffin off for burial, and you will be buried alive.") But *Zumwanda* replied: "I will not since I feel shy." The wife continued, warning her husband: "Look we have now actually taken the path to the grave yard, wake up, otherwise you will be buried alive." But the response remained the same: "No, I will not wake up because of shyness."

A lot of people came for the burial and there was a lot of noice: others were crying, others singing hymns, especially those sang during funerals. The wife tried this and that, but

Zumwanda remained adamant, saying "last time I came back having reached the grave (*dindi*) and this time I am not ready to create unnecessary problems for innocent people who are gathered here." Later on, *bazukulu* lowered *Zumwanda's* coffin into the *dindi*. After that the church Reverend performed his duty: he took soil and declared *"dongo ku dongo, fuvu ku fuvu"* ("soil to soil, and dust to dust") and ultimately requested *bazukulu* to bury the coffin. After *bazukulu* completed the burial process and just before returning home, *Zumwanda's* wife started crying on top of her voice through singing, saying:

> *"A Zumwanda mwaluta,*
> *welani, welani, welani.*
> *Mwalekela njani bana?*
> *Welani, welani, welani.*
> *Mwalekela njani ine?*
> *Nilele uli bana nanjala yikulu iyi?*
> *Welani, welani, welani.*
> *Yikumala banthu*
> *welani, welani, welani*
> *Mwaluta bamoyo chifukwa cha soni.*
> *Welani, welani, welani."*

("Mr. *Zumwanda*, you have gone
Come back, come back, come back.
With whom have you left the children?
Come back, come back, come back
With whom have you left me?
Come back, come back, come back.
How will I take care of the children with this hunger?
Come back, come back, come back.

This hunger is wiping people out
Come back, come back, come back.
You have gone alive because of shyness
come back, come back, come back.")

The people were very surprised to see the widow (*mama wakufelwa*), herself, starting the song just after coming back from burial. They became suspicious that it seemed she knew something about *Zumwanda's* death. They then declared: "confront her!" The widow (*Zumwanda's wife*) later opened up: "Mr. *Zumwanda* used to refuse to do *maganyu* or even to beg for food stuffs from relatives and friends. Consequently, he devised a plan to pretend to have died so that people should make food contributions. That is when he regained consciousness just before burial the first time. When we had finished eating the food which people contributed, I asked him: 'what are we going to do next?' He replied that he would also pretend to die for the second time. But I tried calling upon him to wake up this time around saying 'otherwise you will be buried alive', but to no avail. He maintained his ground that he was actually shy to wake up for the second time. This is how *Zumwanda* has died and that is why I was crying like this," the wife explained.

At this point, people felt very sad about *Zumwanda's* death. People said "if you have been struck by *njala* at your household, it is good to do piece work or even to beg for food stuffs, rather than opting for the route that *Zumwanda* actually followed!

Mama (mother), *gogo* (grandmother) and *bana* (children) enjoying light moments *pakaya* (at home) (photo by author)

Chapter 19
Mama Waseka Uchilima wa Mwana Wakubaba Yekha

Long time ago there lived a woman who gave birth to a healthy baby girl. She lived together with other women who equally gave birth to children. They took good care of their children, giving them proper upbringing. At a very tender age, the babies started to sit (*kukhala*) and later to crawl (*kukhwawa*) as is usually the case.

When the time came for the babies to start walking, all the other babies, except hers, started to walk. Her baby continued crawling. She waited for a long time to see if her baby would start walking too. As a result, when the baby wanted to defecate, the mother used to carry her to the toilet (*chimbuzi*), and would afterwards bring her back from the toilet. When coming out of, and into the house, she also used to carry her daughter.

This continued for a long time until the mother eventually got tired of this task. Eventually, it became clear that the girl was disabled; that she was not going to walk. *"Bakawona kuti tumalundi twayamba kuphapa."* ("They started noticing that her legs started getting thinner and thinner.") The girl started giving all sorts of problems, crying and drawing her mother's attention for no apparent reason (*kumeka*). One day she gave a lot of problems:

"Pala kati pawalo, anyina bakanyamule. Khalepo nyengo yichoko mbwenu kakuti munyumba, balute nako munyumba; nyengo yichoko mbwenu kakuti bibi. Anyina mbwenu balute nako

kuchimbuzi. Bati bawelako nako kuchimbuzi, kakuti nkhukhumba pazuba."

("Whenever she said let me go outside, the mother obliged, she would be outside for a short while before wanting to go back inside the house. The mother then took her in. After a few minutes, she would say 'toilet' (*"bibi"*), after which the mother would take her to the toilet. Just after the toilet, she would say "I want to be outside, in the sunshine.")

Eventually the mother got fed up and confronted her: "You give me a lot of problems. Why don't you walk just like your fellow girls, who started walking long ago? I am tired carrying you here and there! Had it been that you started walking, I would have suggested you go and stay with your elder sister, *Ngoza*, who stays in *Matete* so that you should give me some rest."

Upon hearing this, the daughter felt very sad that her real mother would say all these things to her. Moreover, the place, *Matete*, being mentioned was very far away. She then decided *"pakuti amama ndibo bayamba kuniseka uchilima, ipo niyezge bubo kuluta ku Matete."* ("Since it is my own mother who is in the forefront laughing at my disability (*"uchilima"*), let me try to go to *Matete*, though far away.")

She then got *ngubo* (wrapper) and tied it around her neck. And she later also got a feeding bowl (*nthembe*) full of porridge. *"Wakati nikhwabenge uku nthembe ya bala nibikenge panthazi pachoko-pachoko mupaka nkhafike uku wakukhala mukulu wane."* ("She said I will crawl slowly, at each and every time placing *nthembe* (the feeding bowl) before me until I reach my elder sister's place.") She crawled the whole day, from

112

morning until late afternoon, without her mother following her up.

At night she spent a night at a certain village. Although she did not know the people in this village, they took very good care of her. They felt pity for her. They gave her food to eat. They then asked her: "don't you have a mother?" She replied: "I have a mother, in fact, she is the one who has scolded me (my disability), saying she is tired of carrying me from place to place. She said all my contemporaries are able to walk and why not me?" She further said that "had it been that you were able to walk, I would have suggested you go and stay with your elder sister, *Ngoza*, at *Matete*." "That is why I have been so touched that I have decided to start off crawling all the way to *Matete*. By the way, how near is *Matete* from here now?"

The people felt sorry for her and told her that *Matete* was still a long way from this village. They also suspected her mother to be a witch (*fwiti*). "How can a mother let her daughter, who cannot walk, to crawl all the way to *Matete*?" The next day the girl bid farewell, saying "thank you very much for your hospitality, I am now going." They let her go, saying "thank you, travel safely and may God guide you."

She started off. Along the way, she used to sing:

> *"Nichingeni bala lane*
> *ndandalaza, mama ine.*
> *Amama baninena uchilima ine,*
> *ndandalaza, mama ine."*

("May you feed me my porridge
ndandalaza, mama ine.

113

My mother has scolded my disability,
ndandalaza, mama ine.")

The daughter used to meet people along the way, but they were going in a different direction, and, therefore, could not effectively assist and carry her. The only assistance they could give was to feed her porridge. Once this was done, they used to cover her *nthembe* (feeding bowl) and bid farewell to her, saying "had it been that we were going in the same direction, we could have carried you on our back and drop you right at *Matete*. At the same time, your mother is definitely very evil since this is the first of its kind that a young girl like you should embark on such a long journey and yet you cannot walk, but crawl."

As she continued with her journey, she continued singing her song:

> *"Nichingeni bala lane*
> *ndandalaza, mama ine.*
> *Amama baninena uchilima ine,*
> *ndandalaza, mama ine!"*

("May you feed me my porridge?
ndandalaza, mama ine.
My mother has scolded my disability
ndandalaza, mama ine!")

She continued complaining about her mother's scolding:

> *"Mwana wakubaba bekha ine,*
> *ndandalaza, mama ine.*
> *Nibenge wamusangapo changuba chinthu chinyake,*

114

*ndandala*z*a, mama ine!"*

("I am her own blood daughter
*ndandala*z*a, mama ine.*
If I were a step-daughter it would be understood
*ndandala*z*a, mama ine!"*)

The biggest problem came when she came to a hill (*lupiri*)
was her *nthembe*. Once she tried to put her *nthembe* in front
before her, the *nthembe* could slide back, downhill! She
struggled for a long time with *nthembe*. Late in the afternoon
there came a girl who caught up with her downhill. She asked
her where she was going. She responded that she was going
to her elder sister, who stays in *Matete*, but the she had
problems handling her *nthembe* at this hill – the *nthembe* kept
on drifting down hill, hence she was failing to go past this
hill.

The girl then told her to take heart since she was going to
assist because she was very touched. "Come let me carry you
on my back and we should get going," the girl asked her. She
continued to assure her, saying "once we climb this hill, the
next village that we will be seeing is actually *Matete*." Indeed,
the girl picked her up and took her to her elder sister, *Ngoza*,
in *Matete*.

Upon arrival, *Ngoza* asked the girl: "where did you meet
my younger sister, *Suzgo*?" "I met her at the base of the hill
and she was alone when it was getting dark. I asked her with
whom she was, and she told me she was alone, saying this
was a result of her mother who scolded her disability. You
will get all the details from her after she rests, but as for me I
am going," explained the girl.

Ngoza, the elder sister, was very thankful and, in fact, she gave her *nkhuku* (a chicken) as a token of appreciation for her kind gesture. Since the girl was rushing, she was given this *nkhuku* to eat at her home since she could not wait for *Ngoza* to prepare food.

Ngoza later on asked *Suzgo* (literally meaning trouble) what the real problem was with their mother: "Why could mother let you come all the way to *Matete* on your own and crawling at that? Doesn't she know that you cannot walk?" *Suzgo* answered that it was actually their mother who laughed at her disability, saying "she is tired carrying me around." And she actually said I keep troubling her. "Had it been that you are able to walk, I would have suggested you go to your sister, *Ngoza*, who stays at *Matete*," *Suzgo* reported what her mother had told her. "This touched me so much that I decided to try to come here crawling," explained *Suzgo*. She continued to explain how the girl, a good Samaritan, found her failing to climb *lupiri* and assisted her accordingly.

Ngoza told *Suzgo* that she had to rest for a few days and that, thereafter, *Ngoza* would take her back home to confront their mother. She said if their mother was tired carrying *Suzgo* around, she should have brought her to *Matete*, herself. After two days, *Ngoza* carried *Suzgo* on her back and they started off for their home.

When they arrived home, they found their mother. *Ngoza* confronted her: "Is it true that you said you are tired carrying *Suzgo* around?" The mother responded scornfully: "Why doesn't she walk, unlike all her friends?" At this point, *Ngoza* warned her mother: "stop ill-treating this innocent gift from God, whether he or she is unable to walk, as is the case with *Suzgo*." *Ngoza* continued: "*Suzgo* cannot walk, but this should not be reason for us to take God for granted for He is omnipotent and omnipresent. *Suzgo* is okay apart from failure to walk. It could happen that you can give birth to a baby with two heads, but with one neck. This could not only be a case of disability, but also a mystery (*munthondwe*). Please this should be the last time you ill-treat your own fresh and blood," warned *Ngoza*.

The mother responded, saying "I am thankful for educating and correcting me since there is this saying *"kauzganga ni fwiti yayi, fwiti ni tilinganenge"* ("the one who gives you correcting advice is not a witch or wizard, rather the one who keeps quiet so that you should both face dire consequences of devilish and evil actions"). If it were an outsider, he or she could not have come to advise and correct me so that a bigger thing than this mere disability should befall me," concluded their mother.

Chapter 20
Mwanalume Wapereka Dango Linonono kwa Muboli Wake

Long time ago there lived two people; a man and his wife. This family was very rich. They had seven children; fifty cattle; three vehicles and one very nice bicycle. They had a beautiful, iron-roofed brick house. They also had beautiful furniture, for instance, a display and beds which could not be compared to any other in their area.

They had a ten-tonne truck which used to fetch a lot of money through hiring services. In fact, they did not lack anything at their house - they had all the basics. In addition, the man (husband) had a good paying job with a mining company.

Amongst the items that were in a cupboard (*kabati*), there was a red mug (*kapu yiswesi yadongo*). The husband told the wife that "I am always going to be using this red mug, for drinking water, tea, milk and any similar things requiring the use of a cup. Make sure you take good care of this mug (*kapu*) because the day you will break this cup will be the day when our marriage will come to an end," warned the husband. The wife promised to take good care of the cup in question. Each time she was washing the dishes she remembered to take care of the husband's cup.

One day when she was washing the dishes, an unexpected incident occurred:

"Nkhuku yikafuma pa masumbi mu khichini yikwiza muchanya yili kwelekwele; apo iye wakuti nkhuku iyi yikwiza

119

uheni yinganipala kumaso nisezgeke mbwenu nkhuku yakwapulira
pasi kapu, nakusweka tuchokotuchoko."

("The hen came flying from the kitchen where it was
laying eggs, producing sound *"kwelekwele"*; the time she
noticed that the hen would harm her and decided to duck
(shift) a bit, the hen bumped into the red cup, forcing it
onto the ground and breaking into small pieces in the
process.")

At this point, the wife thought aloud: "this marks the end
of my marriage like my husband promised earlier. She
prepared lunch and waited for her husband to eat. Upon
arrival, the husband exclaimed "my wife, it's very hot today,
before you serve me food, give me drinking water." He was
surprised to note that the wife dilly-dallied and he asked:
"Why are you taking too long to serve me water? Have you
broken the cup?" The wife replied "Yes, the cup is broken."
The husband queried angrily "how was it broken?" Then the
wife explained: "I was washing dishes and while I had your
cup in my hand, I noticed that the hen flew from the kitchen
and headed straight to my face, and when I decided to avoid
it by shifting my head, it bumped into the cup, breaking it in
the process into small pieces."

At this juncture, the husband asked the wife "but do you
remember the promise and rule (*dango*) that I gave you
regarding that cup?" The wife agreed, that she vividly
remembered the caution and promise. Then the husband
explained the way forward: "Now my wife since we
accumulated all these possessions together, I give you the
chance and liberty to choose one item which you think and
feel would help you in your future life. Whether you choose

children, then you are free to get all the seven children. If you will settle for our cattle (*ng'ombe*), currently numbering fifty, then get all of them, whether it's our ten-tonne truck which fetches a lot of money through hire, you are free to get it. Whether it's our *kabati* (cupboard), then you are free to get it, but remember to leave behind the contents, that is, items inside since I have said you get only one preferred item." The husband continued: "but it would be better if you quickly made your choice and left now that our marriage is over. It's not good for you to stay any longer in my house."

Initially, the wife decided to go away with the seven children. But then she hesitated: "I may, indeed, go away with the children, but am I going to take care of them; feed them, clothe them, pay their school fees? Since I am not working, where am I going to get the money for all this? She, therefore, abandoned her choice for the children, saying "in this case, let the children stay!" Secondly, she wanted to get *ng'ombe* (cattle). But she also thought aloud: "I can easily settle for *ng'ombe* currently totalling about fifty, but can I manage to construct *chibaya chikulu* (a big kraal)? What about money with which to pay herders? This will also create problems for me," she concluded. At that point, she also abandoned the second choice.

She then thought about their ten-tonne truck:

"Galimoto yithu ya teni tani yikukaba ndalama zinandi chomene; pala yawerako ku mahayala tikwamba kupenda ndalama seveni koloko mupaka teni koloko zausiku. Kweni kasi na munthu mwanakazi namufiska kugula mafuta ghagalimoto, ndiposo ndalama zakulipira dilayivala namuzitolankhu ine? Njachi yikhale!"

("Our ten-tonne truck brings in a lot of money; after each day's work we start counting the money made from around seven o'clock to ten o'clock in the night. But as a woman, will I manage to operate it, for instance, money for fuel and to pay the driver? No, let it stay!")

Thereafter she thought about *kabati*:

"Kabati withu ngwakutowa kuluska bakabati babanyithu bose kuno kuchigaba chithu, ndipo ngwakuzula na katundu wa ndalama zinadi chomene. Kweni banalume aba bakuti pala nikhumbe kabati katundu yose wamukabati nikhutulire pasi, nilute naye wambula kanthu mukati. Sono ine nadalama zakugulira katundu kuti wazuleso ngeti ni uyo wangubamo zamufumankhu?"

("Our *kabati* is very beautiful; in fact, more beautiful than all the others in this area. In addition, it is full of very expensive items. But my husband is saying if I choose *kabati*, I must make sure that I leave behind all these items and take only the empty *kabati*. So where am I going to get the money with which to buy new items for the *kabati*?")

She the realized that *kabati* on its own, despite its quality, was not important; what made it valuable and complete was the items on it. "Because I cannot manage to buy the items in question, there is no point in taking it," she concluded. The same thought she applied to their modern mountain bike: "If it were traditional bicycles, I could quickly go for it. But these modern ones are a bit complicated. However, the advantage with our bicycle is that I am already used to cycling it.

Nonetheless, the spares are another problem. In any case, tyres need replacing, one tyre would cost a fortune! Hence I cannot take it either," she concluded.

After failing to settle for one thing, though amidst plenty, she solemnly concluded that although the husband had shown some kindness and consideration by allowing her to take one thing of her choice, the husband had been a bit sarcastic in that he knew that she could hardly settle for anything. This was because the husband knew that whatever she settled for needed money to operate and maintain. She came to the painful realisation that she could not choose anything. She decided to express her inner thoughts to her husband through a song:

"Mwa a fumu bane mwayowoyera ukali 'waswa kapu nthengwa yamala'. (x2)

Gonani tulo, gonani tulo, gonani tulo, gonani tulo, nimunyamuleni nilutenge. (x2)

Mwa a fumu bane mwayowoya kuti utolepo chinthu chimoza pera kufuma pa vinthu vyose ivyo tili navyo.

Gonani tulo, gonani tulo, gonani tulo, gonani tulo, nimunyamuleni nilutenge." (x2)

("My husband, you have angrily said 'marriage is no more for breaking my cup'.

Go to sleep, go to sleep, go to sleep, go to sleep, so that I take you away.

My husband you have said 'take one thing of your choice from all our possessions'.

Go to sleep, go to sleep, go to sleep, go to sleep, so that I take you away.")

After she finished singing, she noted that her husband was fast asleep. She then took *ngubo* (wrapper) with which she carried him on her back. But because the husband was tall, his legs could not hang up at her back, but, instead, reached the surface and it was as if the husband was being pulled on the ground: she headed home while her husband's legs were being dragged on the surface.

As she reached her home, her sisters and brothers were surprised to see what was happening. "What has happened with our in-law? Is he sick or drunk?" they wondered. "No, he's neither sick nor drunk," she answered. "But it's his red cup, the one I told you about, that is broken. I told you that your in-law gave me *dango* (rule) over this red cup; that the day I break this cup will mark the end of our marriage," she clarified. She went on to explain to her siblings that, in fact, the cup got broken accidentally as she was washing dishes. She narrated how it all happened as she tried to avoid colliding with *nkhuku* which flew from the kitchen. She went on to explain that, despite it being an accident, her husband maintained his ground, saying that, consequently, their marriage was over.

She then narrated that the husband thereafter gave her an opportunity to choose one thing from all their household property, including their seven children. But she could hardly choose an item realizing that she needed money with which to take care of the chosen item. For instance, since she was not working, it was going to be difficult for her to look after the seven children: she needed money for their food, clothes, and school fees. As for cattle, she would need money to construct and repair *chibaya* and to pay *muliska* (cattle herder). The lorry, again, would need a lot of money for repairs, fuel and the driver's monthly salary. The same monetary problem was applicable if she were to choose *kabati* and *njinga* (bicycle). She told them that that was why she actually failed to choose anything and left everything with her husband.

After this they prepared a place for the husband to sleep since he was still sleeping. They decided not to even give him food for fear of disturbing his sleep. Quite importantly, the wife thought once awake, he would think of going back to his home since he did not even know that he had been taken to her wife's place. As pointed out earlier, the wife picked him to her home after he fell asleep following her song.

Early next morning, the husband got surprised that he was not in his home:

"Ibo bakazgowera kubuka mlenji-lenji kuti balute kuntchito kwambula kuchedwa. Apo bakatenge bazgoke kuti bajinyolore bakasanga kuti mumalo ghakuti matilesi ghati 'dwidwi', kwati mphasa 'teketu-teketu'. Bakazizwa chomene. Pakuti balabiske kuchanya ku nyumba basanga mapaso ghali labalaba. Bakati kasi ni maloto kuti vinichitikire vya ntheura ivi?"

("He was used to waking up very early in the morning to make sure that he was not late for work. When he was waking up, and as he was stretching his muscles, he was surprised to hear the sound of a mat *'teketu-teketu'* and not of a mattress *'dwidwi'*. He also noted that he had slept in a grass-thatched house with poles *'labalaba'* (all over the roof). He momentarily thought 'is this a mere dream?'")

Thereafter, he called upon his wife: "my wife, where am I?" he queried. Instead of addressing her as 'my former wife', he addressed her as 'my wife'. "You are at my home," the wife responded. "How and when did I come here?" quizzed the husband. "I came with you yesterday. I actually had to bring you on my back," explained the wife. "Why should you bring me on your back; was I drunk or sick?" wondered the husband. Then the wife narrated that after she failed to choose one item, as per the husband's decision, she decided to sing a song, which eventually made the husband to fall asleep. And that she then brought him to her home while he was fast asleep. "Now that we are here, who slept in our house, back home?" wondered the husband. "Nobody," replied the wife. "This means all our property is prone to theft!" concluded the husband.

The lesson from this *chidokoni* is that we should not be preoccupied with 'earthly wealth', but we should focus on 'heavenly wealth'. The woman in this story abandoned everything and chose her husband. Similarly, we should choose God and His Son, Jesus Christ, and abandon all the earthly wealth and pleasures.

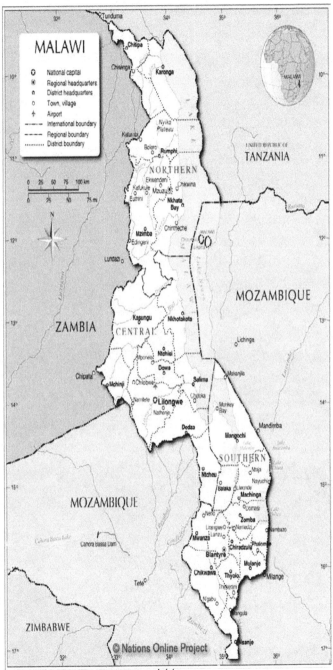

Printed in the United States
By Bookmasters